THE DAY THE ANGELS CRIED

Larry Linam

Larry Linam

authorHOUSE®

AuthorHouse™
1663 Liberty Drive
Bloomington, IN 47403
www.authorhouse.com
Phone: 1-800-839-8640

First published by AuthorHouse 2/4/2010

ISBN: 978-1-4490-5685-8 (sc)
ISBN: 978-1-4490-5686-5 (hc)

Library of Congress Control Number: 2010901083

Printed in the United States of America
Bloomington, Indiana

This book is printed on acid-free paper.

This work is dedicated to the memory of those who died on June 22, 1980 during the worship services of the First Baptist Church of Daingerfield, Texas and the loving, thoughtful, and caring people of this great church and city. You have carried on a Christlike influence and refused to be overcome. Instead, you have chosen to be overcomers for our Lord. God bless you and keep you until we all stand before our Lord and King and sit down together as a family in His kingdom to come.

Your Friend in Christ,
Larry Linam

FOREWORD

Death stands as the world's most unwelcome intruder. Lose a friend, and you feel the pain. Lose a life-long spouse, as I did recently, and you forever struggle with the heartbreaking emptiness and loneliness. But lose a child, and your heart aches forever. Worse yet, if your child dies at the hand's of a murderer, you confront the monster of anger and the protagonist of bewilderment, confusion, and unfathomable grief.

Shocked and astounded beyond words, people in 1980 asked, Why should God allow a sweet seven-year-old daughter of a pastor to be shot to death—and in, of all places, a church Sunday morning service? This book reports the relentless agony of a father who struggled with this question not just for a few months but for decades. This book will bring tears to your eyes as you identify with this man's excruciatingly tragic loss. This book will bring sympathy to your heart as you discern this father's sudden and senseless loss of his firstborn. This book will bring sorrow to your soul as you share the author's deep—seated anger against his daughter's murderer.

How can you forgive someone who has committed a horrific crime against your loved one? How can you turn from the burning desire to wreak revenge on the one who has snuffed out the life of your precious offspring? The author of this moving book shares his intense struggles with these questions.

In discussing these questions Pastor Linam shows how God can help you work through the agonizing weeks, months, and years of losing someone who means the world to you. As you relive the stunning events of that infamous Sunday morning in an East Texas Baptist church service, your heart will be torn asunder. But you will also rejoice, knowing that while nothing can equal death in its unpleasant finality, death can be God's way of opening heaven's door to His own. For as the psalmist put it, "Precious in the sight of the Lord is the death of his saints" (Ps. 116: 15).

Roy B. Zuck, Th.D.
Senior Professor Emeritus of Bible Exposition,
Dallas Theological Seminary
Editor, *Bibliotheca Sacra,* Dallas Seminary's
Theological journal
Author or editor of more than seventy books,
Author of scores of articles and of more than
A dozen gospel tracts

Table of Contents

In Memory of: Men of Valor

Mr. James (Red) McDaniel who died while
attacking the gunman on June 22, 1980

Mr. Kenneth Truitt who died while attacking
the gunman on June 22, 1980

In Memory of

Mary Regina Linam

Mr. Gene Gandy

In Loving Memory
Of
Mrs. Thelma Richardson
Picture Not Available

Heroic Appreciation

Mr. Jack Dean, who attacked the gunman
and was wounded and survived

Mr. Chris Hall who attacked the gunman and survived

Gina and I with her favorite hat, she was a true Mousekateer

The Linam children in 1980, left to right, Jeff, Jennifer, and Gina

Gina and Jeff with Jeff wearing one of Gina's
nightgowns (his favorite picture)

Acknowledgments

As you begin the journey of reading this book, you may literally be gripped by some or all of the emotions that I experienced as the result of years of inner torment. I personally pray that as you read and feel the horror, the hurt, and the disparity, you will remember that our God truly is an awesome God, one deserving of praise and glory. He alone can bring the joy, peace, and blessing to those who are broken, torn, twisted, and agonized by the horrors and traumas of life on this earth.

The world in which we live holds many dangers, which can swiftly bring circumstances that can traumatize us greatly. We must remember, however, that God alone holds the power and mercy we need to experience complete recovery from hurtful, horrible, and traumatic events that can devastate our lives. I have experienced these hopeless and helpless emotions; yet through the love and concern of some wonderful people, God showed me that His purpose and plan for my life continues. Recovery is real and personal, just as God's Word is real and personal. The horror of seeing my daughter lie lifeless on the floor of the First Baptist Church in Daingerfield, Texas, was an event I will never be able to wipe from my mind, but I have continued to recover from its aftermath. At the center of every hurt we experience rings a cry for healing. The healing is found around us in people who love us but is centered in God's formula of John 4:10a, "In this is love, not that we loved God, but that He loved us."

I express deep thanks to several people who will always remain dear to me. First, thanks to my parents for their unconditional love. I have never known a time that Jesse and Irene Linam did not give me the best that parents could offer a child. To them, I say, I love you, and for the rest of my life I shall honor you and sing a song of joy because of you.

Second, I say thanks to all the many friends whom God has sent to encourage me and help me though almost two decades of relentless attacks by hell's forces. My true friends did not judge me but simply loved me as a person. Thanks, Billie and A.J. Booth; Keith, their son; Lois Carr, whom we call Nanny; Cliff and Dessie Covington; Mackey and Glenna Morgan; Gale and Betty Hogan; Jerry and Dorothy Speer; Mary and Olen Crenshaw; Tommy and Phyllis Thompson; and many others who were given to me as blessings from God.

Third I want to say thanks to a very special man of God, John Jones, founder and pastor of the Mountain Top Church, Cisco, Texas. John, when my fellow ministers forsook me during my divorce, you were there to encourage and care for me. I am thankful for your ministry and for your people.

Fourth, "thanks" does not adequately express my appreciation to Curt and Jane Bean, of Amity, Arkansas. These beautiful people loved and ministered to me and to others during and after my divorce. It is clear that your life reflects a love for all people who love the Lord and are in church ministry. Your friendship and many acts of kindness were greatly appreciated and will always be remembered.

It would take volumes to mention every person I have encountered who has given himself or herself to help me at various points. I want you to know that you are in my heart, my mind, and my prayers of thanksgiving.

The greatest travesty of this entire long ordeal would be that if I had chosen to continue to shut out close friends and remain angry, bitter, and indifferent, my life would still be one of mere survival. The important thing to remember is that our Lord does not want us to just survive. He wants us to thrive with abundance.

I could have become a bum on the street, homeless, or a drunk; and people would have excused it because of the severity of my trauma. The most important thing I have found is a peace, joy, and love that I feel spiritually and can verbally express to others as I face each day of my life in spite of the memory of a day many years ago. June 22, 1980, was a day of horror, hurt, screams of pain, and the smell of death followed by years of unmitigated anger along with the "frozen grief" that was a self-inflicted condition.

The "frozen grief" condition rendered me with feelings of uselessness and total disparity. The self-imposed deprivation was a spiritual and mental cancer, which consumed me as a person. I was frozen in time, in my emotions and in my spirit. I cried, "Someone, please help me!" No one could hear my cry because I was too proud; so I locked myself in a prison of "frozen grief."

My memories of looking on the blood-soaked floor and on the blood that flowed from the body of my precious daughter literally hurled me into disaster after disaster for many years. Through recovery I can now take comfort in her eternity in heaven and these words of a song: *"My hope is built on nothing less than Jesus' blood and righteousness."*

When a person is in a state of frozen grief, it becomes difficult for him to reach out for anything. But God sent a friend, a valuable commodity in life, who dared to confront an angry man. Thank you, Barbara.

This book is written with the hope that God will use this work to His glory. The truth is often harsh and unpleasant to us. Circumstances often come to us when it seems that enough is enough. Many times I simply cried out in darkness, loneliness, and utter despair that God would end my ordeal and take me to heaven. I have come to this point many times, but I must say how glad I am that God continued to be merciful to me.

God sees our tears of sorrow, pain, and emotional devastations. *The Day the Angels Cried* is a book bathed in historical significance, the real truth of God's preserving ability, and testimony to the horror that has repeated itself over and over again throughout history.

Do you remember Wedgewood Baptist Church, Columbine School, Virginia Tech, and the events of 9/11? I have been told that my story is too old to tell; but this story is not measured by time but by the awesome aftermath left by these events, the emotional scars on our hearts and minds that cry out for healing and recovery.

People, some of all ages, have died by the malicious acts that are being perpetrated by evil, sadistic, and demented people. I cannot tell you why these people do what they do. But I can tell you that the man who killed my daughter should never have been on the streets. He should have been sitting in jail awaiting a trial on indictment of seventeen counts of incest, three counts of arson, and assault with intent to commit murder. People who live in our communities, from whom we never have a moment's trouble, are sometimes the very ones who commit the horrible acts that devastate unsuspecting people.

God's Word, the Holy Bible, speaks of "the end times" being denoted by a lawless, perverse, and ungodly generation. I believe we are there. *The Day the Angels Cried* is just one of the many proofs of the reality of God's ability to overcome the most adverse circumstances. It is my prayer that you receive knowledge, encouragement, hope, and peace in the midst of life's storms. We are never alone---He is there all the time.

By God's Grace, Larry Linam

Chapter 1 – That Day

Sunday, June 22, 1980, in the East Texas town of Daingerfield, Texas, everyone was getting braced for the heat wave that was supposed to be in the forecast. It is difficult to predict Texas weather, and it was no surprise that meteorologists had missed again. The heat wave had arrived early.

The skies had already given their last blessing of cooling rain ten days before. The heat was already intolerable. The local media network had been warning people in the area to check all of the Freon in their air conditioners and to make sure their ventilation was functioning properly. The ice vendors were working around the clock keeping ice in the convenience stores and supermarkets. People had already made their run on the discount stores within a fifty-mile radius for coolers, summer drinks, and all the protective items necessary to withstand the climbing thermometers, along with the incredible humidity that accompanies East Texas heat. Fewer older people were sitting outside. The ones who would not give up the pleasure of watching the passing traffic from their porches had their fans hooked up and plenty of cold water close by.

I had awakened early that Sunday morning to skies that were rich, deep, cobalt blue. There were no clouds, and none in the forecast. I had gotten dressed quickly. I was serving as part-time minister of music and youth on a temporary basis at the First Methodist Church, and I needed to leave early. I was an early riser because of my job's starting time, so I got up about the same time every day.

I was just about down the steps out of the house when I heard the rush of little feet behind me. Gina, my seven year-old, had gotten up early and proceeded to busy herself getting dressed in her Sunday best. Gina was sharp-witted, always moving with excitement and anticipation. It just did not take her long to get into gear to go somewhere special like church. She loved being around people, and church was her kind of place!

With her hair brushed and her bouncy curls and smiling face with beautiful pearly white, teeth she looked at me with eyes so full of excitement and asked, "Daddy, can I go with you today?" Gina asked again as she came to the door to leave, "Please?"

She knew that it was not her Sunday to go with me, but she thought it would be worth a try anyway. She had nothing to lose. Who knows, I might have said yes. Maybe she just didn't want to face the wild shuffle that was about to take place as the rest of the family began to get things ready to go to church. I was the first out the door, and Gina was always ready to catch the first ride, always wanting to go.

Since I began my work at the Methodist Church, Gina would go one Sunday with me and then the next Sunday she would go to the First Baptist Church, our home church.

"No, Honey. This is not the Sunday you go with me. It's next Sunday," I said as I was leaving.

"But Daddy…"

"Gina, I said no. Daddy's got to go now. Hurry up and finish getting ready. Remember the dollar?" And I went out the door.

"Oh, brother… I know…OK," she said turning from the door with a slight bit of disappointment.

I have realized that just because certain plans are made by parents for their children, the plans do not have to be written in stone. I could have been more flexible.

A seven-year-old whose only desire that day was to go with her daddy. The only thing is, Daddy did not see nor think the way he should have. Sounds like I'm being really hard on myself, but these are real hard facts, not just "what if" facts. I have to live with them every day. The important thing I learned here was not about going somewhere together. The lesson is that I missed the opportunity to say, "Honey, Daddy loves and appreciates your wanting to go with me. I need for you to help get other things done, but remember I love you very much."

Every opportunity to say what you feel about loving a person, big or small, carries far-reaching implications. So many times we just let precious moments escape us. Being a parent is not just coping with the circumstances of our family life, individually or collectively. As a parent, I should have seen the excitement, felt the excitement, and evaluated the simple request on my time. All Gina wanted to do was go with me, hear me sing, be by my side, sit on the front pew, and sing with me. What could possibly be wrong with that request? Oh, dear God, how I have tried to recall or to move time back and say, "You bet, Girl. Get in the truck, but tell them you are going with me." But, sadly, I realize I did not do any of those things that I should have done as a parent, and I cannot move time back now.

So, she did not go with me, but Gina was earning her own money to go to Six Flags the following Wednesday. This was a major challenge for her, and she was so proud to already possess a "pretty fair stash." She got a dollar from me every day for helping out around the house. It was a deal we had made, and usually Gina was very good about upholding her end of the bargain. Therefore helping get her brother and sister ready for Sunday school and church would be a great help and would allow her to earn more money for the trip.

The First Baptist Church had called a new pastor, Brother Norman Crisp, and today would be the first Sunday in his new position. A fellowship was to be held after the services that day, and we had been asked to provide cookies for the dessert table. My thoughts went back to the conversation a couple of days before the church fellowship to welcome the new pastor.

"My, this is fun!" Gina had said with dough on her hands, on her clothes, in her hair, and all over the cabinet and floor. She and her mother were like peas and carrots when it came to doing things like this together.

Gina was one of those excited little people who believed in spreading the idea around of having fun. As a matter of fact, she could scatter stuff all over the place, and this was one of those times.

"Will our new preacher like 'um?" she asked, talking about the cookies.

"Sure, he will, Honey."

"Boy, I hope so. But, if he doesn't can we bring them back home and eat um ourselves?" Gina looked around with that familiar gleam in her eyes.

"We'll see. Maybe so. But I'm sure he'll like them."

Jeffrey was four and a half years old and very elusive, especially on Sunday mornings. He stuck his head around the corner of his door, and gave that sneaky little grin.

"OK, young man. Let's get your clothes on." Gina said.

Then I was reminded of the time when Gina rode her bicycle all by herself to Stephanie's house for the first time. That had been about a year before.

"Daddy, can I ride my bicycle over to Stephanie's?" Gina asked as if there would be absolutely nothing wrong with her request being granted.

A couple years earlier I had taught Gina to ride her bicycle. I had also taught her how to be careful and safe. Gina and her bicycle were hardly ever separated from that time forward. To Gina's way of thinking it was perfectly normal for such a responsible seven-year-old to be able to take her training and put it to good use by riding over to see her best friend. After all, what could possibly be wrong with that?

"Can I, Daddy? Can I?"

"OK," I said reluctantly and bent down to tell her to be careful. Then I saw it! It was the characteristic little gleam in Gina's eyes. "Be careful and call me immediately when you get there! Do you understand?" Well, as you can imagine, I was not going to be too far away. As Gina took off for the three-block ride, I was following on foot behind her. She could not see me and that was fine. What a relief, she was flawless in performance and safety. So I ran back to the house just in time to answer the ringing phone. It was Gina, "Dad, I made it fine. Bye!"

This seemed to be an unusual Sunday morning. As I look back on it, I can remember the conversation with Steve Cowan, who was to teach the Sunday school lesson for our couple's class. The lesson was on how to deal with the loss of a loved one. Steve, a local attorney, was substituting for our regular teacher that day. As he talked about losing a loved one, I recalled a few days earlier, Gina and I sat reading a book when all of sudden Gina looked up at me and said, "I love you."

I pulled her a little closer to me and I also noticed that beautiful twinkle in her eye. "I love you too," I said in a so-proud moment of my life. My thought also drifted a little to think that my life would not be complete without this precious gift.

Nevertheless the teacher dealt with how to cope with the loss of a loved one. He talked about God's sustaining grace. Steve talked about all of the details of a time that is inevitable for all of us.

Steve and I discussed the day and the lesson at length sometime ago. He believes that God was already acting to prepare the hearts and minds of people for what was to be a historical but traumatic event in our lives and in the history of our nation.

The lesson ran overtime because of the class's interest in the lesson. As the classroom door was opened, several kids whose departments had already been released were waiting for their parents. I remember one of my friends said he heard Gina say, "Look what I wrote on the chalkboard today." Gina always occupied herself doing things creative and I can just imagine what must have been on that chalkboard. It is strange when we get in a hurry how we overlook important things about our children. I say this because, before learning the horrible events of that day and before leaving the church, I went back to that chalkboard to see what Gina had written. But it had been erased! It was gone forever! Please, do not miss the little things in your life or your loved ones.

Chapter 2 – **This Is War!**

It was the third Sunday for Norman Crisp as pastor of the First Baptist Church of Daingerfield, Texas. It was a new day with an air of anticipation for everyone who had gathered to meet the new guy in town. The new guy was Norman Crisp, the pastor elect of the First Baptist Church, Daingerfield, Texas. People had come with all sorts of questions. Was he tall or short, skinny or fat? Was he a sharp dresser or just the run-of-the-mill type? Whatever, he was the man of the hour for all who came to the house of God on that beautiful, clear, warm, and crisp day in the small piney woods town of Daingerfield.

The swinging doors that separated the foyer from the auditorium were open, hiding the ushers' pew. This was where the church ushers sat during the service in order to be able to help latecomers or in an inconspicuous manner take care of whatever need might come up during the service.

The head usher was helping people find seats. Because the attendance was large only scattered seating was available. However, Gina had spied her best friend and ran over to sit with her after getting permission, of course.

I recall being told how excited Gina was about having her friend at church and these two were always together like peas and carrots. If you saw one, there was the other. They were together at school, together at each other's homes, and now together at church.

At that time the choir came in and the service officially began. Announcements were made and then the congregational singing started. The new pastor, Brother Crisp, had not made it to the platform yet. There seemed to be some curiosity, which was soon to be satisfied. The new associate pastor, Brother Virgil Fielden, stood up between hymns and informed the congregation that Brother Crisp waited until the last minute before he called to send his deepest regrets. He would not be able to be there because he was home sick with the flu. Brother Fielden told them that it was the first time the pastor had missed church in years, but he just could not make it.

There was a slight ruffle of disappointment among the people, but understanding prevailed. The singing continued as the ushers prepared to take the church offering.

The offering hymn, "More about Jesus," had begun when Gina turned around and winked and smiled at her mother, Cheryl, as if to say, "I love you, and you are my best friend in the whole world."

Gina was a person who could speak exactly what she was feeling by the many different expressions on her sweet and beautiful face. A smile or the twinkle in her eye connected with that unforgettable smile.

The song was in the second stanza. The song, "More about Jesus," was now in its second verse, which says:

> *More about Jesus let me learn*
> *More of his holy will discern*
> *Spirit of God, my teacher be*
> *Showing the things of Christ to me*

Gina was singing this loudly and proudly because she almost knew it by heart, remarkable for a seven-year-old. Also she did not sing in a shy manner. She was loud and proud! The time was 11:20 a.m., right on cue for the ushers to make their way down the center aisle to receive the offerings from the people who had gathered to worship.

It was traditional for everyone to stand on the fourth stanza when the ushers would come forward for the morning offering. There was enthusiasm in the singing that morning. Whatever problems the church might have had in the past seemingly had been set aside as their hearts united in praise and worship. Loudly they sang when they reached the familiar chorus…

More, more about Jesus.
More, more about Jesus.
More of His saving fullness see.
More of his love who died for me.

The truth of this song was about to become more than just words on the page of a hymnal, more than just an old favorite song handed down generation to generation. It was horribly headed toward reality in fear, fight, and unfathomable death and destruction among more than four hundred people singing that song, my daughter, Mary Regina Linam included!

Suddenly and swiftly the swinging doors were kicked open. Some people naturally turned around at the sound of the crash. Standing in the middle of the aisle between the doors was THAT MAN armed with two semi-automatic rifles adapted to full automation by mechanisms found only in the black market, with .38 and .22 caliber pistols and magazines of ammunition carefully taped together for speed reloading, with flak jackets front and back, and with welded bayonets and a steel helmet. The man had carefully and thoughtfully dressed for all-out combat. Immediately after he kicked the doors in, he yelled, "This is war!!!"

Al King was a former math teacher at Daingerfield High School, an educated man to say the least. He held Ph.D.s in math and science from East Texas State University. Yet this man who possessed a level of intelligence was a sexually perverted individual under grand jury indictment for charges of incest filed by his own daughter. He was reportedly under investigation for three counts of arson, and he allegedly as a twelve-year-old child decapitated his own father with the blast from a twelve-gauge double-barrel shotgun.

King opened fire with one of the automatic rifles, spraying the congregation from right to left with as many rounds as the weapons would fire.

Total shock gripped the people at first and everyone just froze. They didn't know if what was happening was real or not. Just three months earlier some young men in the church had put on soldiers' uniforms and had come though the back door to demonstrate a mock communist takeover. Whether the church thought what was happening was another skit or not is sheer speculation. The fact of the matter is they didn't move, and during that time they became victims of a kind of horror that had never before happened in this country. In fact, this kind of horror was that of what real war is about: death, destruction, and fear for life. Faces of faith turned to faces of fear in just a matter of seconds.

Once the people realized it was real and that they were at the killer's mercy, they began to scream and get between and under the pews. Virgil Fielden, who was standing in for the new pastor, leaped to the microphone, and with the most unusual expression of stability in the midst of the most flagrant outpouring of terror, he said, "Everybody get down! Everybody get down!"

God had the right man in the pulpit—a veteran of war, a veteran of life. No one could have faced the situation better; no one could have led the people better.

God knew the times and circumstances of everyone and everything. He had all the right people in the right place at the right time. They were giants who would walk into the face of death and literally fear no evil—men of valor, men of faith, and examples of godliness as well as greatness. From the pulpit into the pew—God is solid, sovereign, and faithful!

Mr. Jack Dean, serving as an usher, was the first to confront King as the doors opened and the shooting began. Jack reached for the barrel of the rifle and just as soon as he grasped the weapon, King fired, sending a massive explosion of bullets and fire into Jack's right hand and arm, knocking Jack to the floor with blood and smoke around him. The shooting continued until Chris Hall, a young man who had been operating the sound controls behind the swinging doors on the left side leading into the auditorium, literally threw his body into the door, knocking the gunman back into the foyer. Chris, a former football standout and a guy known to have an ability to move fast, instinctively followed the gunman and found himself face to face with a .38 caliber pistol. King began shooting at Chris as he darted and dove down the stairs to the basement, which were on the left side of the foyer. The bullets were hitting so close to Chris that his body felt the wind. He sensed that he would never get away. But miraculously, he made it to the basement without being hit. Wood was being blown off the railings of the banister and mortar was being blasted from the walls. The bullets were flying and bouncing from wall to wall.

When King missed his rapidly moving target, he kicked the doors in once more and headed for the main body of people for a second time. Like a raging bull and roaring lion, he came to deal death on a massive scale, having over four hundred rounds of deadly ammunition ready to fire in an instant.

Smoke and screams filled the air.

"OH GOD...HELP US! HELP US!"

"I'VE BEEN SHOT...I'VE BEEN SHOT!!!"

"PLEASE STAY DOWN!" Brother Fielden spoke over the microphone. "STAY DOWN! PRAY!"

As Al King tried to enter though the swinging doors once more with only a single motive on his mind – TO KILL – his automatic rifle jammed. Already, the two largest men in the church were running up the aisle toward the back door. Red McDaniel and Kenneth Truitt, two of Daingerfield's most respected men, furiously collided with King as he moved toward people. Two giant defensive ends going after an opposing quarterback on fourth down with everything at stake do not even compare. However, this situation was far from football. These men were literally guarding their families and protecting the entire church full of people with their lives.

It is my firm belief that all these men knew exactly what had to be done – and they did it. I remember reading in the Bible that love knows no fear. I found this in 1 John 4:18, "There is no fear in love." This perfect love was evident in the lives of the people who stood up to the present evil and acted in faith and love.

When Red and Kenneth hit Al King, they knocked him into the foyer again. Only this time King, who was a fairly large man himself, was wrestled completely to the back wall in an effort to get him out of the church. The three men literally busted out a panel of a door as they crashed through to the outside. During the struggle King lost his glasses, and was semi-blind without them. Even though both Red and Kenneth had King bear-hugged front and back, King still managed to manipulate the use of the .38 caliber pistol and shot both "Red"

McDaniel and Kenneth Truitt at point blank range. One died instantly, and the other died about an hour later. Nevertheless they accomplished their task. Had it not been for the sacrifice of these men, along with Gene Gandy, the usher who was killed as he met King coming in the door, and Chris Hall, it defies the imagination what the assassin could have done as he unleashed the malignancy of the devil himself. From all appearances and calculated plans, King came ready to kill the entire congregation. He had an arsenal of firepower that included over four hundred rounds of high velocity cartridges, with the massive killing power of a .30 caliber weapon.

After King was outside the church and obviously knew that his plans had been thwarted, he threw the .38 caliber pistol down after emptying the rounds into Red McDaniel and Kenneth Truitt. He ran around the corner of the building and across the street to the fire station, where he just stood on the sidewalk, waiting and watching for the next victims to appear.

Another young man rushed out of the church, picked up the rifle that had been dropped, rounded the corner of the building, and saw King across the street. He dropped to his knees in a military firing position and began to squeeze the trigger over and over in the midst of his shock and tears. He was not aware that the rifle was the one that was jammed and was not firing. King pointed another of his weapons at the young man, but never fired.

The killer turned to run, stumbled, and fell. He had the .22 caliber pistol in his hand, and when he fell, the gun discharged with the bullet barely piercing his head. He fell and was immediately surrounded by some of the men from the church. The police had not yet arrived.

From the time the doors were kicked in and the "declaration of war" began, a Sunday that would live forever in the memories of those present, until the time King fell on the ground just outside the fire department was approximately FOUR MINUTES. Four minutes of fear, the fear of being under attack! The terror and the horror that left families and friends scrambling to see if everyone was okay. Four minutes when faith was shaken to its core! People crying, screaming, and clamoring to find a safe haven that did not, for certainty, exist. Yet in those same four minutes the truth of life and death revealed itself for the whole world to see over the next few hours as history was made and seen in this great country. Never had mass murder occurred during a public worship service in the history of the United States.

Everything happened so fast that what was remembered as just a blur in many minds has painfully been blotted out of others but not from my mind. It will most likely stay with me forever.

Chapter 3 – Horror in the House of God

I would never expect the house of God to look, smell, or feel like a war zone, but the inside of that church did.

The look of stark fear was expressed by widened eyes trying to catch any movement of the still present danger. The only obvious sounds being heard were those of sobbing, soft muffled cries for help, and people calling out for God's protection and help.

People began to get up from beneath the pews. Screams and cries permeated the air like a battlefield scene of wounded soldiers calling for a medic. Brother Fielden, the associate pastor, did his best to keep the people from coming to a full stage of panic. He knew that more harm could come by innocent people who were frightened beyond description.

"If you cannot help, please move to the outside through the doors at the front. Please stay calm. For those of you who have been wounded, you will be attended to as quickly as possible. If you have a family member who has been shot, please gather around them and pray. Let's pray and stay calm. We need God at a time like this."

He kept on repeating these words. God's man was speaking with holiness to confront the obvious evil in the house of God and to bring assurance and comfort.

Cheryl was still under the pew when she looked up and saw Stephanie screaming, "Gina! Gina!"

Stephanie would look down at Gina and then look at Cheryl. Then she would scream and cry in a tone filled with horror. Again she would look down at Gina, and then at Cheryl. She looked back and forth with a face of fear and horror, crying out her best friend's name. Her best friend was not answering, not moving, no response at any point.

Cheryl still did not believe the events of the past seconds, and it was not clear what Stephanie was trying to say. Then, terrified, she remembered seeing Gina go down. At the time, Cheryl thought that Gina was getting down like everyone else. Now, it suddenly dawned on her that Gina had not yet gotten up. She would not get up to sing the offertory hymns, she would not sing "More about Jesus," nor would she stand again with any congregation. Cheryl looked and could see nothing but Gina's little navy blue shoes. She grabbed Jeff and shoved him out from under the bench where she had been protecting him with her body.

Panic-stricken, she crawled out herself, and in one quick maternal move she was up under the pew where Gina was. She could not see her head, so she grabbed her feet and slowly pulled Gina toward her in order to help her up. When she did, it became horribly unbelievable but obvious that Gina had been wounded in the head.

So many things flashed through her mind in those next few seconds. There had been thousands of little cuts and scratches throughout Gina's seven years on this earth, and she had always come to "Momma." A band-aid, a kiss, and a word of encouragement would always soothe the malady. As she lay there patting Gina's legs, all she could say were these words. "It'll be alright, Honey. It'll be alright! Oh! Gina, it's gonna be all right."

They were words of unmitigated horror and confusion carried by the horror that filled God's house of worship.

"God! Is this a joke? Things like this just don't happen! Not in America! Not in Daingerfield, Texas! And certainly, not in your house! Is this a joke, or what??"

But it was no joke! It was the stark reality of just how evil and mean the world has become and is today. The horrible facts of this story have been relived numerous times, such as the shooting at Wedgewood Baptist Church during a youth fellowship, the awful shootings at Columbine School in Colorado, and the recent tragedy on the campus of Virginia Tech. The looks on the faces of people directly affected by these horribly tragic events are a constant reminder to me as I have looked on the expressions of fear and hear their words of hurt and the emotional damage.

She looked back down at Gina to see if what she was experiencing was real or not.

"God, let her be OK. Please turn back time and don't let this happen. I'll do anything. She can't be hurt. She has her money for Six Flags, and they are going next Wednesday!"

She looked down at Gina one more time and realized that this was not a joke. Gina had really been shot. Stephanie's uncle, Tommy, rushed over and grabbed Cheryl by her shoulders and began to gently shake her calling her name.

She looked into Tommy's eyes and said, "She's been shot. Gina's been shot!"

Young Jeff, who had been wandering around, hearing the cries from pain and watching the confusion of the scene, ran back and pulled on Cheryl's coat. "Help me! I'm scared!! Is Gina OK?" The indelible mark of all the death and destruction hits the mind of a five-year-old just as severely as it does an adult.

"Yes, Jeff, Gina's gonna be fine. Gina's OK." She knew she might not be telling our son the truth, but Gina was still breathing, and there was a ray of hope. She had overheard a doctor say to a young couple years before, after the couple's son had been in an automobile accident, "When there's breath there's life, and when there's life there's hope." She had never forgotten that.

"Please stay with Gina! I've got to go get Larry!" She said pleadingly to Stephanie's uncle, Tommy. "Please stay with Gina!"

Cheryl did not want anyone else to tell me before she got to me. Gina was our daughter, and to her it was a very personal thing. Besides, she didn't know how I would react, and she also knew that she had to get Jeff out of there.

Cheryl held Jeff behind her and headed for the door. She didn't know at that time if it was safe outside, because she still didn't know that there was only one man. When she had hidden under the pew, all she had seen was the barrel of the rifle when King stuck it through the door. She never saw him. All she knew for certain was that Gina had been shot and that she needed to get to me as quickly as possible.

When Cheryl and Jeff reached the front door of the church, she heard one of the large men who had wrestled King to the outside. He was sitting on the ground to the right of her crying, "Oh! Oh! God help us! God help!" He had been shot in the heart. It was Kenneth Truitt. Just at that moment several men rushed to his side and immediately began caring for his needs, which were great. Three bullet holes dotted his chest. Time has not erased the bloodstains on the sidewalk from my mind. I doubt if it ever will.

I have heard about the term "closure." Since that day, the years that have gone by have not proven this term correct in my mind. I can still see the expression of fear on Kenneth's face, the expression of the pain within his large body as he lay on the concrete walkway. The closest feeling of closure in my mind has come only in accepting the facts that occurred on a day of historical significance. It was the first time in the history of this nation that mass murder had occurred during a public worship service. The word "closure" seemed so remote then and still is to this day, because the scenes of these events are indelible on my mind and heart. I cannot put these things in a closet, shut the door, and forget them. I think about them every day. I live with the lessons learned constantly, and I am acutely aware of people around me every time I find myself in a public gathering. I am not afraid of my feelings or surroundings. I just accept the fact that I never know where an ever-present evil may come to rob, steal, destroy, or even kill innocent, God-fearing people. The small sense of closure comes in the fact that I go on with my life with a true sense of purpose to do God's will. To me, this is closure.

Cheryl had to step around another one of that heroic duo, Red McDaniel, who had died during the fight, in order to get out the door and into the car. She still didn't know what had happened or who had done the shooting.

When Cheryl and Jeff arrived at the Methodist church, Cheryl parked immediately in front of the building and ran up to the door and entered. Knowing that a person should not be disruptive in God's house, she was trying to think of how to tell me without interrupting the services. Still her feet did not stop moving. She went down the left aisle toward the front, approached the side of the platform, and called my name. If whispers could be screams, she screamed in a whisper, soft but penetrating to my ears.

"LARRY!"

The Methodist pastor saw her and the look on her face. I turned and saw the same face, which was exploding with fear, and said, "What is it?" I was almost afraid to ask. But I knew it could not be good. I knew that it was not like Cheryl, a calm, collected, strong individual, to come up to me like that in the middle of a service. And she was as white as a sheet.

"What is it?" I repeated to her, but with a great deal of force that seemed to shake her into a soft voice but one of devastation.

"A man broke into the First Baptist Church and shot a bunch of people! And he shot Gina! Larry, he shot Gina, and she's been hurt real bad!"

I literally fell to my knees, where I cried out to God.

"No, God! No! No!" I cried loudly.

"Come on, Larry. We don't have time to waste. We have to go! Now!"

The people knew that something terrible was wrong, but they didn't know what. Then the pastor came instantly to my side and asked, "What's wrong? What's the matter?"

I removed my choir robe while Cheryl told the Methodist minister the same story she had told me. Then the minister announced this to his people. There were families who were part of both churches, so some of the people quickly got up and left. The rest stayed for a time and prayed.

Daingerfield, a small East Texas town, nestled in the piney woods where life had gone on for decades with a live-and-let-live approach, held close family ties. Some families had strong worship ties to the Methodist church while some of the same family's members held strong connections to the Baptist faith. The family member of the Methodist church held on to the same faith in God as did their Baptist loved ones.

The denominational differences did not detract them from their love for each other.

A friend came up to me and Cheryl and said, "Come on, Brother! I'll go with you!" I left instantly and headed for the Baptist church.

As Cheryl and Jeff were getting back in the car, Gina's first-grade teacher, a member of the Methodist church, came up to her with tears in her eyes and told her that she would go with her.

"OK," Cheryl said. "Get in!"

"I'll be glad to drive, Cheryl!" Susan said.

"No. I need to stay busy. Susan, Gina's dying," Cheryl said softly. She had got to a point of despair. She was a true lady of action and she focused on the needs.

"Oh no, Cheryl, be positive. She'll be alright," Susan said. She was crying hard. She was trying to be reassuring to Cheryl.

"I want to be positive, Susan. But I know that Gina's dying."

Shortly after Cheryl said that, they rounded the corner and saw the virtual mass of people who had gathered in front of the church. By that time the police had roped the entrance off, and ambulances were headed toward the scene from nearby Mount Pleasant, Hughes Springs, Pittsburg, and Omaha. The Daingerfield ambulance was on a run at the time of the shootings, and was not available until later.

My friend from the Methodist church and I got out on the opposite side of the street directly in front of the door. Some of the key people saw me as I got out of the car and began to move toward me to try and restrain me from entering the building, while another close friend from my Sunday school class, came up on my right side and grabbed me around the neck. He hugged me and told me that Gina had just died.

"No!" I thought, as I continued to try to imagine what would cause such a terrible thing to happen. "Gina has done nothing to anyone—she is only seven years old! Seven-year-olds do not die sitting in a worship service!" None of this was making any sense.

All of this was happening so fast that it became total mental chaos. I began moving to the front door of the church to get to my daughter as fast as I could. At least three more of my friends, joined by the Chief of Police, Jim Keene, attempted to block the entrance. My adrenalin was pumping so fast that they couldn't stop me.

"PLEASE, GET OUT OF MY WAY!" I said as I continued to move forward, dragging all four men.

"Larry, you don't want to go there! You don't want to see your daughter like she is now!" said the Chief of Police. I remember that Jim's eyes were stern and his face like stone. But that didn't stop my progression. I was going in.

All of a sudden, I looked up over the crowd and shouted, "WHERE IS THE MANIAC WHO SHOT MY DAUGHTER? I WANT HIM! WHERE IS HE?

The chief spoke calmly because he knew that I had been deeply hurt and was literally full to overflowing with rage and anger. "Larry, we have already taken him to the hospital. He's gone."

I never took my eyes off of the door, and never stopped trying to move toward it. Oh, how the element of fear was driving me closer to those doors. Doors that would open a vision of pain and sorrow for years to come that would stretch my world to a breaking point. The rage was physically driving me while the anger was motivating my thoughts.

Cheryl had just arrived and saw me struggling to get to Gina.

"Has Gina died?" She asked one of the men.

"Yes, Cheryl, I'm sure Gina is dead." The answer was definite and final.

Cheryl, like a wounded warrior, put her hands to her face and began to crumble. It was at that very instant that God intervened in the life of Cheryl and spoke to her heart clearer than she had ever heard Him speak before. I can recall her testimony as to what God spoke to her. "It's alright, Cheryl. She's with me." God's power and grace overwhelmed her. She lifted her face from her hands and said softly, "It'll be alright. Gina is with Jesus. It'll be alright."

Cheryl then walked up to me and said, "Larry, you really don't want to see Gina like she is. Please remember her the way you left her this morning."

I looked deep into Cheryl's eyes. I remember hearing in times past that the eyes are the windows into the soul. The emotions within me were churning with a mixture of intensity that I had never encountered before. What expressions were coming from deep within my soul began to manifest themselves outwardly much like times when I had played a football game that demanded a strong defense and hard-nose hitting and explosive reactions. Yet Cheryl's eyes seemed to convey a deep inner sense of fearless calm and composure.

Cheryl saw my face, and it dawned on her that if she were in my position, nothing would stop her from seeing Gina either. In an instant, I was gone and already at the two entrance doors that had been broken from their hinges. I was moving closer and closer toward the most devastating scene that a father, parent, and human could ever witness. Cheryl was not far behind me.

Cheryl turned and went in the church. When she did, the men stopped struggling with me and let me go. I entered what was absolutely and undoubtedly the most horrific episode of my life. I was not fearful of what I wanted to do, but of what I could not do.

I eased through the door and into the aisle. I could hear Virgil Fielden still praying. I knew that we always sat on the left, but I immediately looked to the right and saw Gina's blue shoes and little body that had been covered with an astro-turf matt. It was at this moment that I began to realize that my visual and mental awareness was beginning to slow down. I was seeing for the first time a place that no parent thinks he or she would ever see. I was experiencing an awesome sound of quiet refrain. It was as though I had entered a very holy abiding place that demanded a sense of stillness and reverence like never before.

I walked closer, looked beneath the pews, and saw that Gina's hand was covered with blood. I saw the puddle of blood that surrounded her and realized that the devastating message delivered to me only moments before was a horrible, horrible reality. I dropped to my knees with my head in my hands. I knew that Gina was dead. I never lifted the cover. I had seen victims of gunshot wounds to the head before. Never, ever would I have imagined this but the truth was undeniable.

Not believing what was before my eyes, I sat down on the ushers' pew in the exact same spot part of my family were sitting when the shooting started. I didn't know that at the time. I just sat there, looked down at Gina, and cried. I began to weep without and within myself. My body and soul felt as if I was being emptied of life itself.

"I love you, Honey," I cried softly. "I love you." I could not stop the onslaught of tears.

I looked down and to the right as Cheryl gently knelt down beside our daughter. Cheryl looked at me and said, "Larry, God has Gina in His hands and she is alright." I just could not imagine things being "alright." I was listening but failing to comprehend all this.

While I sat on the ushers' pew that Sunday morning, I was filled with every kind of negative emotion possible for a man to experience— all compacted into a few brief moments. Guilt… shame… a great sense of loss… defeat… violent anger… incredible grief… hatred… bitterness… total dismay…revenge.

I felt like my entire being was on fire from the ferocious lightning storm of memories that quickly moved across my brain. I thought of all the times that I should have been with Gina. No chance now! I remembered her little arms as they reached out to me when I finally came home, only to be brushed aside with the problems of the day. I would never feel them again! I knew how deeply she loved me, yet I really never acted much the same way to her. There was nothing I could tell her now! I hurt. Oh, how I hurt! Death had come to Gina, and now it was swiftly flooding over me. The elements of a traumatic experience such as this were moving me into a realm of shock that I had no way of dealing with at the time. I wanted to just lie down and die; yet I also wanted to live to exert vengeance on the perpetrator.

Larry Cowan came up to me as I sat there and said, "I'm so sorry, Larry." I looked up and saw Gina's little boyfriend's dad, the boyfriend she had kissed in the coat closet at school. I didn't say anything; I just nodded. I had no adequate words in me. Besides, what was inside of me, I knew, had no place in a house of worship. But this place looked like a slaughterhouse.

As I was bent over one of the daughters of my dreams, one whose life had been senselessly taken away, Brother Fielden came over and prayed with me. Then an emergency medical team came in, along with a few of my friends, and said, "Larry, would you please step outside? We need to take Gina."

I just sat there.

"Come on, Larry," Cheryl said. "There's nothing more we can do here."

I realized when she uttered those words that it was over. There was no turning the clock back. Gina was gone to be with the Jesus she loved so much. She was so full of life, making every moment count. It seemed like Gina Linam lived seventy years compared to seven.

There would be no more smiles, no arms reaching out to greet me with a huge hug; no more "I love you, Daddy." There would be no more excitement about getting into my truck to go somewhere with me. All of this beautiful life was gone from my physical existence and would only remain in my memory.

I got up with an emptiness that was darker than any dark I could ever imagine and walked outside. Frank Berka, my good friend and the owner of the Ford Dealership where I worked as the service manager, saw me and headed straight for me. He had heard the tragedy on the radio, and came immediately to find me. Frank was probably the only one who could have handled me at the time. Frank's temperament had just the right mixture of "velvet and steel." Added to that, I hold Frank Berka in the highest esteem to this day.

Frank just seemed to assume control, and took me into the church offices so that I could call my folks. When I called my parents there was no answer. I then called the local funeral home in my hometown of DeKalb, Texas. The director was a lifelong friend, and I knew he could locate my parents and tell them to call me as soon as possible.

Noble Bates, the funeral director, found my parents eating out at a local restaurant in DeKalb. In 1960 Mr. Bates had buried my brother, Charles, my parents firstborn son, who had died of cancer. Mr. Bates was always accessible. While I was in college, I experienced a head-on collision auto accident. It fell to Mr. Bates to find my parents and deliver the news that their son lay in a Little Rock, Arkansas, hospital with serious head injuries and possible paralysis. It just seemed that bad news fell on Noble Bates to deliver at times. However, there was never a more qualified and gracious man in the area that could do this than Mr. Bates.

When my mom saw Noble coming toward their table, as they were eating in a local restaurant, she said, "Oh, tell me it's not Larry this time!"

Noble said, "No, Irene, it's not Larry." He paused. "It's Gina." The pain I feel just to sit and write those words sends tears rolling off of me. It's a tender spot when I have to realize that my life was to be never, ever the same. My mom and dad immediately made their way to Daingerfield.

The emergency medical personnel suggested that all the families go to the local hospital in order to have their vital signs checked. No one wanted any more death, certainly not if it could be prevented. As I sat in the chair in the trauma center of a local hospital, nurses, doctors, and emergency medical people hastily moved around me. People were being attended to, including me. I am sure that some form of shock and awe was on my facial expression, but my thoughts were becoming more about revenge and anger as time moved on. Little did I know that across the hallway and down one room the man of harm lay under guard. Had I known he was there, that man would have died where he lay, without any doubt, fear, or hesitation on my part! Whether he was conscious or not would have made no difference to me. He was a killer and the most disgusting human on the face of the earth in my eyes. In fact, unaware of his presence, I walked within a few feet of this child killer and did not recognize him.

Frank drove us to his home where I had decided to wait until my folks arrived. He told me that with all of the news helicopters and television crews moving in and reporters swarming the area that we sure didn't need that. And he was right. Media mania had begun and the entire world would know about the incident before evening.

While I was at Frank's home, Frank and I stood on the patio. There was not much being said by anyone. After all, what do you say to someone who has gone through an ordeal of mass murder? The fact is that the shock and trauma had stolen our words, but just the presence of friends spoke volumes to me. However, a few minutes passed, and

I asked to be alone on the patio. Frank made a move toward the door, and my friends followed him.

Now it was just me on the patio—alone. As I sat there just looking into the clear blue summer sky, I noticed one small cloud had appeared on the horizon. The forecast was sunny and hot with no mention of rain. The cloud appeared in the southwest and moved straight toward me at an unusual pace. The cloud grew closer to me; it became obvious that it was huge in size. The closer it got, the larger it grew and became as black as the darkest and deepest blue. No rumbling of thunder, no lightning, just quiet darkness in the middle of a hot afternoon. The cloud had become so large that it seemed to cover the entire city of Daingerfield. I just sat there watching the cloud as it ceased its movement and just seemed to hover over me. There was no wind, no noise, just darkness.

Quite suddenly, it started to rain with the sun still shining. This was not in the forecast. I got up and looked up at the sky. Much to my surprise, there was only that one large black cloud directly over Daingerfield. The rest of the sky was completely clear. It started to rain and Frank came out and said, "Larry, you better come in, Looks as though it may come a downpour."

I said, "I've never seen raindrops the size of the ones falling. They must be at least five inches in diameter."

As I entered the kitchen I looked at Frank and said," You know I guess the angels of heaven are crying with me today."

It rained hard for a few minutes and only over the city of Daingerfield. It did not rain again until late August. A few minutes of rain, and then the cloud completely disappeared. In most cases a cloud usually moved on in whatever direction the wind blows, carrying the rain with it. I believe, however, that this was not an ordinary rain cloud. This was not a freak cloudburst on a hot, summer day. This was a message from God that said, "I weep with you just as I wept over Jerusalem." The angels were among us, above us, and around us. The cloud did not move on—it just went away. It was a message delivered from the heavens to the hearts that were broken and shattered by grief!

The rain stopped. The crowd had gone and all that remained were sorrow, sobs, and grandparents in Frank Berka's home. I received word that Gina was being transported to Bates Rolf Funeral Home in DeKalb, as I had requested. What lay ahead was to become the most revealing facts that I had ever faced as a father. I have had to face many difficult circumstances as a man, a father, a husband, and a minister but nothing like the hail storm of decisions coming toward me.

CHAPTER 4 – A FATHER—A FUNERAL—A FAILURE

I sat in the car driving toward DeKalb, knowing that just a few minutes before a hearse carrying the body of my firstborn child had traveled this same highway. The thought hit my mind, "She should be sitting right behind me cutting up with my son, Jeff." The thoughts coming to me were like a flood. An old saying crosses my mind that speaks volumes: "You don't know what you really have until it's gone."

My family should be headed to DeKalb to have a visit with grandparents, to play in the swing, to enjoy a family dinner, or even watch a golf tournament on television while children play outside. Instead, I was headed toward a funeral home, the same funeral home I visited as an eleven-year-old child when my older brother died from cancer. I had made this trip many times but not under these circumstances. It was like the car was on autopilot in an airplane guiding itself along a pre-chosen heading. I was just along for the ride. However, the thoughts that were cascading through my mind were more along the line of getting this horrible feeling of anger resolved by taking care of a murdering individual in a manner that would be suitable and worse than I was feeling.

I pulled up into the driveway of my parents' home in DeKalb to find that word had spread quickly, because a large number of cars were parked along the street in front of my parents' home. News of events like this travels fast. As I approached the house, I noticed two of my best friends coming toward me. One of them was Steve Coulter from Lockesburg, Arkansas, and the other was Curt Bean from Amity, Arkansas. Both had heard the news of the church shootings from newscasts on radio and television. The reality really began to move in on me at this point. Why would two of my best friends be at my parent's house in DeKalb, Texas? They were both businessmen, and their Sunday is a time to relax and share time with their own families. But I knew they were there for me. The greeting was bittersweet. The facial expressions on our faces were those of hurt, dismay, and unbelievable sorrow, yet with just the right touch of hugs even among three big men.

After greeting my friends with an appreciative comment, I turned and moved into my parents' house only to see it filled with friends of my parents and with a sensitive hush. The television was on, and all eyes were fixed on the screen. I then heard the voice of the news anchorman, Dan Rather, say, "And now an update on the latest events of the mass murder in Daingerfield, Texas."

I turned to see live pictures and news reporters standing where I had stood just a few hours ago. The scene was people standing around just looking inside the auditorium with men and women removing pews and carpeting. The cleanup had already begun. The news commentator then began to speak of the carnage that was so obvious, and as he spoke about the victims, the television screen was filled with pictures of those who had died as the result. My eyes focused on the TV screen, and suddenly they enlarged and placed Gina's picture taken of her in school. I just could not believe that all this information could get out this fast. For the first time it was beginning to sink in. "She is really gone! They're talking about my precious daughter. Where did they get the picture?" Little did I know that not too far behind me was an onslaught of news media looking for me or anyone else that could know the particulars of the event.

Caravans of people began to arrive from places that I had served as pastor, until there was no more room in the house. My dad then moved us to the back part of the house away from visitors and television newsmen. Just as the house filled with people, every television channel was filled with reporters, cameras, and interviews about a tragic day in the history of our nation. Even I was not aware that this was the first time in our history that mass murder had occurred during a public worship service.

The telephone rang, and my dad picked it up. I heard him say, "Thanks, Noble, we will be there within the hour." Then he hung up. As I stood there in silence, my dad came to me and said, "Son, in a few minutes we need to go to the funeral home to take care of some arrangements so that Noble and Robbie can proceed with taking care of Gina. OK?"

I acknowledged him with a nod of agreement as I turned away to sit down in a chair in the back bedroom. I knew what he meant, but I began to think I should be outside pushing Gina in the tree swing, not going to a funeral home.

The time was crawling by as the time came to leave and go into town. As we pulled up in front of the funeral home, I noticed Noble Bates and Robbie Bates standing in the doorway. I had played football with Robbie in high school and had maintained a good friendship with him through the years of separation. Robbie greeted me with a hug and tears in his eyes to match mine.

As Robbie grasped my hand he said, "Larry, I am so sorry to have to see you under these circumstances." He then opened the door and motioned my dad and me inside.

I then heard Noble say, "Larry, come down here with me." I followed him down the hallway into a room filled with caskets. It was at this point that I faced another reality of Gina's death. I was not picking out a birthday gift, looking for some pretty outfit for her trip to Six Flags, or planning our next fun-in-the-sun event. I was going to choose a casket in which to lay the body of my precious little girl, my firstborn child.

Mr. Bates began to explain to me in a soft and gentle voice, "Larry, each casket has a description of the product, services, and costs on the card placed on top. You choose what you feel you want and don't worry about the rest. We'll work though this later."

I just stood in one spot looking around the room filled with caskets. I looked at colors, cloth, pillows, and *costs*. I realized then that I could not even afford to bury my own child. The numbers on the card spoke volumes to me. It was like they were screaming at me "You are a failure!" I had failed to protect my child from danger; I had failed to give her my love and attention; and now I could not even succeed at giving her a decent funeral!

I turned and looked at my dad, and he knew my feelings better than anyone. Some twenty years before this day he had stood in the same room picking a casket for his firstborn son, my older brother Charles. My dad has always been there for me with the right temperament and advice, and this was no different.

My dad spoke to me, "Son, do not look at the price. Just pick what you want Gina to have. Pick one and don't worry about anything else."

Without speaking a word to my dad, I looked at the faces of Mr. Bates, and Robbie and decided to leave. I was defeated in the distress of the ultimate failure of life. The feeling of complete worthlessness was flooding my heart and soul. I turned away and left the room while pointing to the casket in the corner to my right, "That's fine, Noble. Get things ready."

Robbie stood beside me outside with his arm around me, not saying a word, just being the friend he had always been and still is today. As everyone came out, I moved toward the car as I heard Noble tell my dad, "Jesse, we will have Gina ready for viewing in the morning. Come back around 10:00 a.m."

Over the next two days I spent hours just sitting at the funeral home. Time was passing slowly for me when I wished it would just fly away.

Two days passed, and the third day I sat in the den with a few friends, dressed in my best suit, about to do something no father wants to do—go to the funeral service for one of his children.

As the limo pulled up to the front of the First Baptist Church in DeKalb, Texas, I was shocked! People were standing outside, covering the entire front lawn, down the steps, and around the side of the church. Inside the auditorium, every seat was filled, on the ground floor and in the balcony. As we started up the sidewalk steps, it was then that I began to hear the shutter lenses opening and closing on cameras. The media was there in full force. ABC, NBC, and CBS television crews and commentators were speaking softly as we approached the church entrance. I thought, "How could they do this!" But the truth was evident. This was an event that had gripped the heart and soul of America, a seven-year-old child killed in a house of worship. I moved on like they did not exist. After all, I was not there for them. I was there doing the final act of love for Gina, for tomorrow I wouldn't be able to see her body ever again on this earth.

As I looked around the vast assembly of people, Mr. Bates stepped to my side and softly spoke to me, "Larry, I know that your concern is strictly Gina and your family; but just so you know, many people care about what has happened, many state and national representatives are here to honor Gina's memory along with all the others. They hurt with you today." He was correct in every sense. Legislators from Austin, our state capital, congressmen from Washington D.C., and celebrities from different entertainment fields had come to pay their respects to Gina.

I took my seat on the second row near the casket, just looking at the most beautiful display of floral sprays I had ever seen. The music began with Gina's favorite song, one she would sing with me many times, "I've got a Mansion just over the Hilltop." She would always sing it proudly. I could not sing this time. It just seemed to be missing something. I was told that the last song Gina sang was "More about Jesus," the song she sang just before she was mortally wounded. The thought crossed my mind as I looked into the open casket, "Now Gina knows all there is to know about Jesus. She's there with Him, but I would prefer that she was here singing with me."

The funeral proceeded as I sat and drifted in and out of awareness of what was being said by Reverend Virgil Fielden, our associate pastor from Daingerfield. Then it was time to leave and proceed to the cemetery. The news media was not allowed inside the church, but outside they waited ready to capture the attention of a nation as a child's casket came through the doors. I moved my son Jeff and my daughter Jennifer quickly into the limo, knowing that I had to shelter them as much as possible.

The procedures of funerals were well known to me. As a pastor, I had conducted many different types of funeral services. I knew that soon the end would come, and everything concerning my ability to remember Gina from visual perspectives would occur at the final look into a casket at her lifeless body. So, here I was, a father, many times too busy to give adequate time for a ride or a walk or to sit and read stories, grasping every second with my eyes. I realized ultimately and finally that I had failed a big test—my test as a father to my loving child.

Chapter 5 – The Bentwood Rocker

Several months had passed since the funeral and the emotions in me had escalated to a level that had me embattled beyond measure. Yet something kept pulling at my heart to tell someone what was inside of me. The opportunity to meet with a man, a well-known Christian seminar leader, sparked in me the thought and interest in writing a book to reveal and relate the true circumstances of what had happened in real life to me. So I made the call that would set me on a course and task that would bring some release to me, or so I prayed.

The conversation began. "This is Larry Linam. How are you doing?" I said softly.

"Fine," he replied. "You barely caught me. I'm getting ready to hit the road again tomorrow with a seminar that runs for two weeks. What's up with you?"

"I need to visit with you today—this afternoon if possible," I said with a hit of urgency in my voice. "Would that be convenient?"

"Sure. Come on over," he responded and gave me directions to his home.

He didn't know me at all, but there was something that seemed compelling to him about my need to talk. He was not prepared for what was going to happen, nor was I for the most part. After all, it could not hurt just to meet and discuss the chain of events and a few personal feelings, could it?

I arrived a short time later, and following the usual cordialities I sat in one of two bentwood rockers in his main living area. I looked intently into his eyes, and his curiosity began to rise concerning what I was going to say. Very slowly I started. I said, "There's something that I must get off my chest before I really get going on a book."

"I am all ears, Larry," he said as he sat down on the floor.

"It may take some time. I really don't know where to start."

"At the beginning," said my friend.

"OK. Let me back up to the first week of October, 1977. I know it's pretty far in the past, and that you didn't know that I existed then. But," I sighed, "that week marked the beginning of years of deep rebellion against God, and I remember vividly just what happened that started it."

He could tell that it was not easy for me to communicate the depth of my emotions. It sounded more like the beginning of a confession that had long been overdue. He just sat there. There was no dialogue. He made no snap judgments. He was just a listening ear.

"I surrendered to the full-time ministry in 1969," I said.

"So did I," he replied. Yet what he said did not interrupt my train of thought.

"I had great expectations of just what God wanted me to do in His kingdom. But I had come to the place, after nearly ten years of service in various churches, where my family literally existed with no food in the house. I felt like a total failure as a man and a provider. To top it all off, the church where I was pastor refused to listen to me concerning our needs. Do you understand where I am coming from?"

"Yes, I do," he assured me.

"In case you think I was a horrible spender, please consider that I was trying to live on less than eight hundred dollars per month before taxes. The church gave me no gasoline allowance, but they expected me to visit in homes and hospitals at least twice a week. This kind of struggle had been a problem in every place I served since entering the ministry. My dream had become a nightmare."

"Couldn't you share your needs with the church, Larry?" he asked.

"I'm getting to that."

"Sure. I don't mean to butt in. Go on," he whispered.

"Let me give you an example. Our refrigerator was on the blink, and the serviceman said that it was not worth fixing. We could not afford another one. So, in order to make some extra money to purchase a refrigerator I began to haul hay for a local farmer. He had agreed to pay me eight cents per bale stacked in his barn. I did this for three nights beginning at 10:00 p.m. until 3:00 a.m. the next morning. I made enough to purchase the refrigerator."

By this time I was becoming visibly upset. It was like a mighty river of hurt was about to overflow. My friend reached in his pocket and handed me a new handkerchief.

"Now, make no mistake. I was completely exhausted by the Sunday morning following my hay-hauling experience, when one of my dear deacons made the comment to me that he didn't think I should be working two jobs. He didn't believe in the pastor having two incomes since I was in the professional ministry. This man continued to attack me behind my back until a collision course was set.

"It is my desire that you understand the depth of that former situation as a man of God, and how I felt when I looked at his insurance agency, broiler farm, three hundred acres of soybeans, and registered cattle for commercial marketing. To me, it was like the pot calling the kettle black."

"Sounds like it to me. Did the rest of the congregation feel like he did, or was he on a one-man crusade?" he quietly asked.

"I never went out one-on-one to find out," I said. "I was very proud and unusually aggressive about the work of the church, and for this man to tell me what he did was very offensive to me!"

I began to wrap the handkerchief around my hands tightly, from one hand to the other. My body language was telling him that the dam could break at any time. What kind of flood would come? How deep were the waters of pain and anger? How tempestuous is the sea of life?

I continued, struggling to hold back. "This was the time when I knew that the devil was getting through. He had constantly fought me, but I was beginning to feel an anger swell up inside of me that I had never been faced with before. I mean from a ministry point of view, you know?" My voice was beginning to gain in strength and volume.

"I can say categorically, I know! Go ahead," he spoke with an intensity of encouragement.

"Well," I proceeded, "I knew that only God could work on my heart to keep me from getting extremely bitter. I knew all of this in my head, but when I saw my loved ones hurting because of my being underpaid, I decided it would be easier to take the deacon's flack rather than stop hauling hay. Believe me, hauling hay made me feel even more like a failure at the time. I just didn't know any better. I didn't stop to think that God doesn't make any failures. Nevertheless I believed that the church should pay me enough salary to do the work that the Lord called me to. Was I right or not?" I waited for his answer.

He replied, "Larry, you were biblically right, but let me go on to say that I do not know all sides of the issue." He spoke with as much objectivity as he could master. By this time I was beginning to tear his handkerchief as I relived the utter despair of not being able to deal with the issue.

"At any rate," I continued, "I felt like an utter failure. I felt as if I were sneaking around behind the backs of the membership and doing something that was wrong. I know that was not the case and deep down inside I knew it at the time. Nevertheless I had never known such a feeling of failure, and it didn't fit my thinking. I felt as if I had been robbed of my time to study the Word of God and of my priorities. What was going to come first—my tie with my family, the work of the church, or my time with God?"

"Larry, it sounds to me like a classical case of burnout," he said.

"It was, but there was much more than that. Let me finish before I stop short of getting it all out. I perceived myself to be a total failure. Yet I was going around visiting the hospitals, calling on the entire membership of the church at least once a month, and watching the attendance rise from 136 in Sunday worship to 325 in less than six months. My thinking was completely inconsistent with what was really happening. In other words, my mind had already accepted the fact that I was a failure. I couldn't rise above the attack of Satan to destroy my mental processes through this one man. Fourteen new converts were baptized into the fellowship of the church, but this still didn't stop the destruction."

He responded, "Maybe you should have ignored him, Larry. I know that's easy for me to say, but it sounds like the church was going great; and you and I both know that there will be opposition when that occurs."

"Oh, I know that now. But back then, I was full of pride and put myself in a very awkward position by letting the devil get me to the point of saying that it was either that deacon or me."

My voice began to quiver and weaken, but I could not decide if the cause was from the hurt or the anger, and I surmised it to be a little of both. As I continued, the arms of the bentwood rocker were becoming looser. I didn't care. For a moment it was as if I were desperately trying to go back in time in order to change it. Then I looked at him with tears welling up and continued my story. Tearful and scared, I was doing something that I had never done—I was getting real!

"Brother, I have never really let all of this come to the surface, but I feel like I must. You see, I was tired, confused, and disappointed in my calling. To be completely honest, I was just plain mad at all Christians."

"I can't say that I blame you," he said. "But I believe you are not using the term Christian correctly, if by that you mean people like that deacon," he replied.

"Maybe," I answered, "but I began to have questions literally spring up in my mind that shook me to the bottom. My perspective at the time did not let me see clearly at all. To me, all church members did not care about their pastor, let alone his family. I mistakenly saw them all like that deacon. Let me give you an example of how clouded my thinking had become because of my deep hurt. A friend of mine, who was not even a member of the church, came to us and told us that he wanted to buy my kids some winter clothes. It was October, and winter was about to set in. I didn't have a dime to buy Gina as much as a coat. She was attending school in summer shorts with leotard hose to keep her legs from getting cold when she went outside to play with the other kids," I said with a broken voice.

I just could not contain myself any longer. I burst into tears and physically tore that handkerchief to shreds—as well as the bentwood rocker. He was seeing my pain as it gushed out, as the pieces of furniture hit the floor as well as the pieces of a shattered life. I could not mend the dam. My mask had completely washed off. Larry Linam was opening up. To this day, I do not believe that I intended for that to happen. But isn't our God great? I needed to let go of all the logjam of emotions and let loose the flood of tears streaming down the river of my life.

"Please do not be embarrassed with me, Larry. Let it go. Whatever needs to be released—just let it out." His words were chosen very carefully.

"Oh, my friend," I said with tears streaming down my cheeks, "I went into a terrible state of anger and rebellion against God. I would get furious."

As he listened to my story that day in his home, he saw what pride could do to a person when allowed to run its full course. But this was just the tip of the iceberg. There was more to come! There was more to release—years later.

"Larry," he said softly, "I determined at the beginning of the conversation that I would try to offer any counsel that could be helpful. However, to be perfectly honest, I sense you're headed toward something that has been eating at you like the most serious cancer imaginable. Why not open up completely so the inner healing can at least begin to take place?" We were eye-to-eye, head to head. This was serious!

I waited a moment and said, "I have never told anyone what has really happened inside of me since Gina's death. After my friend bought my kids their winter wardrobe, I began to take a careful look at myself and at my situation. I was defeated, and I knew it. My old nature was in control of my life, and my fellowship with God felt nonexistent. I had all of the earmarks of a total breakdown."

Beginning to cry again I continued, "The month of October 1977 brought about more pressure than I knew how to describe. It came from the church, my home, and most of all from my personal expectations of myself. Things literally began to collapse around me. This wasn't supposed to happen. I stood in the front yard of the parsonage one night and faced the biggest battle I had ever faced up until that point. I knew that I had not been able to prepare myself spiritually to do battle against the evil one. I stood in my own distress and discouragement, knowing that I had come to the end of my rope. I was afraid of what I might do—literally afraid. I was not clothed with the armor of God, nor ready to fight in his power. I was naked and ready to fall, and fall I did."

I paused and held my head down for what seemed like several minutes. I took a deep breath, and said, "You see, Brother, I had asked the budget committee to have a specially called meeting to approve a raise in my salary from $150 per week to $300 per week, plus a gasoline allowance for visitation purposes. Does that sound extravagant to you?"

"No. Not with that size of a congregation and the number of people in your family. Not at all," he said.

"Well, it seemed reasonable to me too. I was waiting for the meeting to get over so I could tell the family that God's people would meet our needs. The budget director walked up to me and informed me that the committee had decided against the raise. They were willing, however, to recommend to the church that a loan from the church savings account could be made to us in the sum of $300 with a payback being held out of my weekly check. This church owed no debts! The savings account was fat with several thousand dollars. In the nine months I was there, the worship attendance, which at first was between 70 and 100, had increased to 226. Ushers were having difficulties seating people in both Sunday services. The prospects were numerous. Excitement was building. And the committee wanted to make us a loan so that we could eat!" The volume of my voice had increased greatly as I shared this story of a spiritual nightmare and the devastation that laid to waste one more man of God, one more ministry of harvest for the Lord.

"What did you say?" he asked, earnestly endeavoring to bring me back down.

"I refused, and in the intense stress of the moment, I told the chairman of that committee something I thought I'd never personally say. 'As of in the morning, I quit. You can tell the committee that the services in the morning will be dismissed at 11:50 a.m., and my resignation will be effective at that time.'"

"This was on a Saturday night, right?"

"Right."

"And you resigned the next day?"

"Yes. I got ready for church, and I left a little early so that I could type out my resignation before anyone got there. That was the saddest day of my life up until that time. I can't tell you how frustrated, angry, and defeated I felt. I was not only leaving the church, I was leaving the ministry altogether. After the chairman of the committee left that night, I stood in that yard and shook my fist in the face of God. I told God that if that was the way I was going to be treated, He could forget about me ever preaching again."

I was tearing at the handkerchief as the tears streamed down. My new friend could do nothing but cry with me. Then it dawned on him—I was blaming Gina's death on my personal rebellion against God. I stared out the window for several moments without saying a word, feeling the weight of my emotions pressing harder than ever before.

"It took several trucks and trailers to load our worldly possessions and head out for a new horizon. From that point forward things have gone downhill. I started working at a steel mill and hanging out with the boys. I worked two jobs. I became a workaholic. I never saw the kids. I moved from one place to place another. I was always working, working, and working. I had determined that I would be completely independent and self-sufficient."

45

I paused, and then finally came out with it. I looked my friend in the eye and asked, "Did God take Gina because of my rebellion three years earlier?" It was the one question that had haunted me for a long time. It was the question for which I had no answer. It was a question that had robbed me of my inner peace, joy, and serenity. It was a question riddled with guilt and torment.

He didn't know what to say. I had such agony in my eyes that he couldn't bring himself to answer at all.

"Well, did He?" I asked again.

"Larry," he spoke cautiously, "I don't know. I can't answer that with a degree of insight. I do know that God does not take rebellion lightly."

When he said that, I put my face in my hands and cried harder. He had not moved from that spot on the floor for over two hours. He still could not move. God was not through dealing with me. The handkerchief was shredded, the bentwood rocker had lost most of its screws, but God was present in the room that day.

The agony in my heart and mind is sometimes an overwhelming thing. The existence of rebellion toward God, the painful loss of my daughter, and now to have to face the awesomeness that God may deal with me in a very severe way. Although God's hand of judgment was on me, I also felt His mercy. But as for the handkerchief and the bentwood rocker, they would have to be replaced with new ones.

The truth appeared to be that because of me, I had lost my precious and beautiful firstborn child. How could a man of God, a father, be so blind and insensitive to life that he would turn his back on an almighty God? I did! Now the stage seemed to be set to "pay the price!" It is God's way of tempering justice with mercy. I realize that I did not cause her death. I also know that Satan was using this to just depress me and to literally destroy me to a suicidal point in life. I realized the full depth of description of Satan as a "robber, thief, and a killer."

CHRISTMAS WITHOUT YOU

The years have come and gone like the wind
The time has passed like a river flows with no end.
It seems that you have been gone for only a short while
But more than two decades has not dimmed you smile.

Oh, I remember that precious face that glowed so bright
How it brought joy to me when I came home at night.
My day could have been long and tiresome at best
But that sweet smile would bring comfort and rest.

As time goes on, I can do just fine thru the months of a year
I work, I play and live life without fear.
But Christmas comes and I see faces with joy
As little boys and girls expect their favorite toy.

They run and jump excited as they can be
But I live with the pain of you without me.
Or is it the other way of me without you
It does not matter, the emptiness is still true.

I know that life must go on from day to day
But somehow I long for you in my own way.
Since 1980, the year that you went away,
I think of you as I live each day.

But when Christmas comes and families gather round
I am left here with your memories that are profound.
I turn aside from all the things that I have to do,
And think of your love and
CHRISTMAS WITHOUT YOU.

Love Dad, Dec. 2001

Chapter 6 – The Trial

Nine months passed after that terrible Sunday in June. And during those months I became more angry and fearful. Thoughts of the days ahead weighed heavily on my mind. My mind was consumed with the events of the past, such as the funeral, the friends who had come to my side and helped with funeral expenses, and the many failures I had faced in my life up to that point.

On the day of the final competency hearings for Alvin Lee King, I did the normal things to make myself presentable to the world and sat down to breakfast. My expression was mixed with excessive intensity and controlled rage. It was the day of the final set of competency hearings for Alvin Lee King. As I sat in a breakfast grill with some friends of mine, there was some casual talk among us. The conversation between me and them was somewhat solemn due to the incredible pressure that I knew this day was to hold—especially for me. Eventually the talk came around to the hearing to take place and what could happen. The talk had been that justice would be served one way or the other. I said, "Guys, let's change the subject of the conversation."

"We'll cross that bridge when it comes." I said with a voice that was calm but with eyes full of revenge. I had had nine months to do more than weep over the situation. I had stopped crying, and anger had set in. I was calm on the outside, but I was a raging bull on the inside. I was angry not at my life, but rather at the time this morning and at the careful moving from place to place of a man who had murdered people.

I told the guys good-bye and that I would catch them tomorrow morning.

I walked out the door and headed for the Morris County Courthouse. The charges for the bizarre, yet obviously premeditated, murders of five people, as well as the wounding of ten others, would be discussed in court during the next few hours. Was Al King insane, or did he literally calculate the horror that he caused on June 22, 1980, in the First Baptist Church of Daingerfield, Texas? This would be decided today.

For eighteen months the people in the community, as well as the entire nation, had speculated and debated the outcome of the judge's decision today. Did King have the mental capacity to stand trial for murder?

From the viewpoint of the people, the months, days, and hours since the tragedy were like a funnel—broad at the top and narrow at the bottom. All of the murders were already committed. All of the funerals were over. All of the pain and bitterness had taken deep root. All of the conjectures of the media, who were completely incapable of knowing the real feelings of the families and of the town, had been heard. All of the lawyers' arguments and manipulations could go no further. All of the previous hearings had finished. THIS WAS WAR! It all came down to this day. This was Al King's day in court. This was Daingerfield's day in court. This was all of the surviving family members' day in court. This was my day in court, and justice was going to be done!

I prayed as I drove. "Oh, God! Please give justice. Please do not allow this man to be set free in society. Please keep these deadly desires in me from surfacing when I see him. I cannot handle this day. Oh, God! If I have ever needed You, I need You now!"

I vividly remembered the first competency hearing, which occurred in September of 1980. At that time I was still employed at Berka Ford in Daingerfield. The car continued its path toward the courthouse, but my mind went into reverse. As I traveled back in time, I recalled Al King being taken to John Sealy Hospital in Galveston for extensive surgery and medical treatment immediately after the shootings. He was then transferred to Rusk State Hospital, in Rusk County, Texas, for mental evaluation and further treatment. I recalled how King had seemingly received preferential emergency treatment on the Sunday morning of the shootings. I thought of how I and the other families had virtually competed for doctors and ambulances. And now King was to be returned to the scene of the tragedy in order that the district judge, B. D. Moye, could make his ruling as to King's competency to stand trial. Judge Moye's ruling was to be based on the Morris County Grand Jury's indictment, which required professional and legal opinion as to King's competency. That was why King had been kept in Rusk State Hospital.

No one really knew when King would be returned to Daingerfield for the ruling, but the indictment had been filed in Morris County and so the decision had to come from there as well.

I remembered how I wanted to talk to Sheriff Joe Skipper about the status of King's evaluation and just happened to stop by the Morris County jail one day for an informal visit. The District Attorney's office was silent. So I thought that my friends at the courthouse might offer some relief or some answers.

When I arrived at the sheriff's office, the back of the jail was congested with welding equipment, trucks, and other items of construction. As I entered through the back door, I immediately saw someone I knew.

"What's up, James?" I asked.

"Hey, Larry," James said cautiously. "We're beefing up the security for Al King."

"That's for sure!" I said as I surveyed the construction. "It looks like the C.I.A. is bringing up public-enemy number one. When's he coming?" I thought I might find something out from unofficial sources.

"Don't know," said James without stopping his work.

"Know where the sheriff is?" I asked.

"He's somewhere around. Came through a while ago," replied James.

"See ya."

"Yeah. Be careful, Larry." James paused and looked at me as if to say more, but he didn't.

I was literally shocked to find that the workers had to work around the clock to get things ready in time for King's return. I noticed that my friend was supervising his entire welding crew to add heavier bars to the cell block where King was to stay—alone!

To my amazement a huge, steel-plated door was being constructed, separating King's cell from the regular cellblock corridor. As I began to think of the extreme cost of just the steel adjustments being made, I also noticed a telephone crew and electricians installing a closed circuit television system and monitoring devices.

I began to calculate in my mind the money being spent for just one man. Make no mistake—I did not think of King as just another man. However, he WAS only a single individual, and all of this was being done just for him. As I thought about it, I knew that five welders would make a collective wage of $125 per hour. I could not imagine the expense of the extra material and electronic equipment. My immediate reaction was anger. It looked like they were trying to keep an entire community out instead of only one man in. The truth of the matter is they probably were.

As I stood in frustration rooted in utter rage, the sheriff came around the corner.

"Hello, Larry. Can I help you?"

"I just wanted to talk to you, Joe. I was trying to find out something about King's status."

The sheriff stood silent for a moment. Then he took me into his office and expressed his deepest concern for me. He began to reassure me that there was a very strong case against King, and that he was almost sure that he would be competent to stand trial sometime in the near future.

"Is Al King going to come back?" I asked with thin lips and gritted teeth.

"Yes," said the sheriff. That was his only response as he looked deeply into my eyes trying to perceive my thoughts.

Joe Skipper, the county sheriff, was a man of few words, and his simple answer ended the conversation about Al King. The rest of our visit revolved around casual things. I was not able to probe any deeper as to when King might be returned. If the truth were known, it was better that I couldn't find out anything further. However, I later found out that King had been brought back the very night after that day when I was standing in the cell where he was to be kept. King was brought in secretly between midnight and two in the morning.

The hearing took place very early in the day and lasted only twenty minutes. King was in, out, and gone before anyone in Daingerfield even knew that he was there. But this time everyone knew that a murderer would come to trial.

I was completely lost in thought, remembering the events that had preceeded the day in court, when a car pulled into my path, quickly bringing me back to the present. I honked. I continued toward the courthouse.

As I drove, I could not stop the flood of memories no matter what I did to stay current. My mind immediately went back to how my family had been struggling financially. I tried to weigh the extravagance that I had seen being spent on a killer against my own situation and that of all the others who had been hurt, in order to make some sense out of the entire nightmare. I couldn't.

Through the constant hum of road noise, the past kept creeping in. My thoughts were a kaleidoscope of Gina, Al King, and my own future as a father, my bitterness, and my fear that King would be ruled incompetent and get off scot free. I thought of what it would be like if I had only let Gina go with me that Sunday and of the anger, confusion, and everything else that had consumed me for the past eighteen months.

I thought of how the bills had piled up over the months and of the sacrifices that everyone was experiencing because of my emotional upheaval and bitterness. I remembered how my anger had risen to a boiling point when I realized that I did not even have the money to bury my own daughter and had to depend on the gracious gifts of loved ones and friends.

My memory took an extremely painful trip back to the time when Gina had to go without warm clothing because I could not afford them on the salary the church paid. We barely got by. As much as I cared for and ministered to the members of the church I served, they did not adequately provide for my family and me. My love for them remains intact to this day, but the truth is the truth. I later found out that Steve

Coulter, one of my best friends in Lockesburg, Arkansas, was one of the men who helped pay for the funeral.

The crown of irony and the epitome of failure as a father came to a head on the day of the funeral. It wasn't just the lack of money. Thoughts of every other provision that I should have given—but didn't—rushed to the forefront of my mind. My time… my guidance… my attention… the expression of love… everything!

As I continued toward my destination, I could not put out of my mind the funeral home and the humiliation I had felt. I realized that I did not even have the money to do the last thing right.

Then I thought of how many taxes I had paid and of how much all the families that were affected on that Sunday must have paid over the years. It became increasingly clear that the victims had been victimized in more ways than one. I remembered once again how the murderer had been rushed to Tyler by ambulance and then immediately to John Sealy Hospital in Galveston for brain surgery. But it did not stop there. King was being kept under strict psychiatric supervision following the extensive brain surgery paid for by my taxes. He was being fed, clothed, and housed—again, all from taxpayers' money. I had seen with my own eyes how an entirely separate section of the Morris County jail had been remodeled just for him. My rage was unbelievable.

I remembered returning to work after seeing the work on the jail.

"Where have you been, Larry," asked Frank Berka, my employer and one of my closest friends today.

"Out," I said, trying to avoid telling him.

"I know where, Larry. You shouldn't go to the jail anymore. Just stay away. I understand something of how you must feel, but it will do you no good to keep asking something you cannot find out until the time comes."

"I know," I answered softly. Frank was good for me, and I knew it.

The reason it had become advisable for me to stay away from the Morris County jail and Justice Center was for self-preservation. I had crossed a line in my heart and mind. My heart was broken and so saddened that I fell into the most depressive state and I had been physically ill several times. However, I had become greatly concerned that justice might not happen. To me, justice could only be one thing: death for Al King. I had become so obsessed with killing a man who in the eyes of many deserved to die that I had come very close to taking his life. The scenes have played through my mind many times since.

I had gone to work as usual but on this particular day something much unexpected occurred about nine o'clock. As I walked out of my office at Frank Berka Ford in Daingerfield, someone called my name. "Mr. Linam," said a voice from behind me. I turned around but saw no one that I knew or that I thought would know me. Two men started walking toward me and stopped very close to me as one spoke. "You don't know us, but we have come to take care of this man who killed your daughter."

I replied, "Sir, I don't know you or your names or where you came from, but I firmly believe it is in our best interest that you go back to where you came from and let us take care of our own problems."

The two men had divulged a bit of information that gave me a window of opportunity. The opportunity to kill Al King! Quick – easy – it's over! Their visit was real, but I began to fantasize. The thought of taking matters into my own hands did not come to me until I discovered that Al King and his mother were wealthy people. And they had retained the services of the second-best defense attorneys in the United States.

Fear came over me when I learned that the defense was to be insanity. So I had an answer! A 30.06 rifle with a finely adjusted telescope, a rooftop overlooking the jail's rear entrance about three hundred yards away, and an early morning daylight arrival time for Al King. I had all the information I needed to work with, the emotional motivation, and a tall ladder to get into perfect position.

The time was right. King arrived at the rear entrance of the jail just about daybreak. King, cuffed and shackled, moved methodically out of the car and toward the jail entrance. Six law officers completely surrounded him as he was escorted to the jail from the transport vehicle.

I could do this only if my aim was precise and King came back out with a gap between him and the officer behind him. I knew the gap would occur, because I knew the door was a single door just wide enough for King to pass through it to the outside.

Inside the jail, the competency hearing lasted only twenty minutes. So I got ready.

Sure enough, in a few minutes the door opened. As I looked through the scope, I could see a man wearing a white shirt and a pair of handcuffs standing about two or three feet inside the doorway. The gun was up. My aim was calm and steady. I was ready to do it!

The first man out was the police chief in Daingerfield and a good friend of mine. He stopped just outside the door, looked around, turned, and motioned for King to come. King did not walk straight or upright thru the door. He turned sideways and bent over at the waist. Two more officers stepped up beside him. My frustration became very intense. I was ready. I was poised—but I was also denied. I really thank God for this now. I had missed an opportunity to become what King was—a murderer.

I just folded up on the rooftop and cried. Then I climbed down the ladder and into my truck. A couple of minutes went by, and Al King was gone. He was returned to Rusk State Hospital for further testing.

I returned to work and to my thoughts. The recurring thought was, "My last chance is gone—my chance to avenge—my chance to even the score!"

The months passed, as I knew they would, and time was approaching for the next competency hearing. But this time was to be different. It had been leaked by very reliable sources that the doctors had recommended that King could be found competent to stand trial. The trial could take place, and hopefully justice would prevail.

All these things were flooding my mind as I headed for the Morris County Courthouse on the day I had been awaiting for eighteen months. Alvin Lee King would either be declared competent during the next few days or he would be declared mentally incompetent and would be a lasting drain on the very people he fully intended to kill, an unforgettable yoke of bondage to their emotions.

Fear of the possibility of King's freedom in due time had already begun to grip the community. Statements such as, "We don't know if we have strong enough laws to convict this man" and the like, had circulated during the funneling process. To add to this fear was the presence of Percy Foreman. He was a famous lawyer and one of the most successful defense attorneys in the country. He was retiring from the practice of law and in my judgment wanted this feather in this retirement cap.

This was not only the day for Al King to be judged. It was the day for Daingerfield justice and the last case for a "big-time" legal mind. It was a day that would set a precedent, not only in the field of law but also in the lives of everyone involved.

All thoughts of the past immediately left as I pulled up to the south side of the courthouse. The security was extremely heavy at each entrance of the building and all over the adjacent parking lots. People were being frisked with metal detectors and pat-downs at the doors on each side of the courthouse.

I had a reason for paying close attention to the security. I had a knife—a knife of dagger proportions. I drove around the courthouse, looking at each entrance as well as for a place to park. Two officers at each door were doing a pat-down. I looked at one of the entrances where I saw a set of female officers. The one place a woman officer would not touch a man was the groin area. That would be my ticket! That was my door!

I had assumed that metal detectors would be used to check people before they entered the courthouse. I also knew that as the father of the deceased victim I would be permitted into the courtroom and given a reserved seat, one of my own choosing. The district attorney had chosen to charge Al King with the murders separately, seeking to stack the sentences. The trial would begin today for the murder of the seven-year-old girl, Mary Regina Linam, my daughter.

I got out of the car and headed for the door and the two female officers. The media were out in mass and were circling like vultures. When they saw me, they pressed me for a comment with their long-range microphones. I stepped briskly to the door at the front of the building.

"No comment! No comment!" That was my only response as I pushed through a mass of media.

As I arrived at the door, my eyes met the eyes of one of the officers as she spoke. "Hi, Larry." She was one of the county sheriff's deputies with whom I had become acquainted when she bought a truck from Berka Ford.

"Are you sure you want to be here?" she asked.

I replied, "Gina, would you want to be here if you were in my shoes?"

Nothing else was said. She began the pat-down by asking me to spread my legs and lift my arms. As she moved the metal detector over my shoulders, under my arms, then down the sides, she stopped at the waist. The next thing I heard was, "Larry, I hope you change your mind." The metal detector did not sound!

I was in—and no alarms! What an idea! The idea was so good I could not believe how easily it worked. The knife was taped between my legs, held by a thin layer of scotch tape. Why didn't the metal detector detect it? The knife I carried was made of wood! I had used a soft pine block of wood and fashioned it on a cutting lathe. I had sharpened it to a point. It is hard to imagine, but the blade was sharp enough to slice a sheet of heavy bond paper. It was also sharp enough to cut skin and pointed enough to stab easily.

I entered the left side of the courtroom because that was the side where King would be seated. I wanted to be on the front row so that when Al King came in I could look him squarely in the eyes. I wanted him to feel my pain, sorrow, and rage. A rage so fervent that if looks could kill—he'd be dead! Looks that would speak the words, "This will be your ticket to hell! Where you belong."

The sheriff of Morris County met me as soon after I entered the courtroom and shook hands with me. He led me to the third pew behind the railing that separated the trial area from the viewers' gallery. Finally he spoke. "We saved this whole pew for you and your family. Are they here?"

"No, just me," I answered and took a seat in the middle of the third pew. No one was allowed to sit on the first and second pews.

The sheriff returned to his seat near the judge's chamber door. While he was walking to his seat, I reached down with my left hand and pulled the tape loose from my leg and groin area. The knife slid down my pants leg and into my western boot.

Perfect! I was set and ready!

A voice behind me and to the right spoke, "Son, could I sit here beside you?"

I replied, "Sure, Lady, it's a free country."

I never paid any attention to the woman because my mind was focused on one thing—sending a demon to hell where he belonged! I didn't even notice that the woman was my own dear mother.

The next thing I heard was a man's voice on my left as he sat down next to me. "Hello, Mr. Linam. My name is Brantley Foster. I'm with the Texas Rangers, and I'm here to help you through this ordeal." A big man to say the least, and I knew he was a man who meant what he said.

I looked down beside me and there was a pearl-handled, .45 caliber pistol. The name of this Texas Ranger had become well respected in East Texas. He was known for his strict adherence to carrying out his mission whatever the cost might be. It had been stated that he would arrest his own mother if he had to. I'm not so sure about that, since I have gotten to know him much better. We are now very good friends.

Brantley had been assigned to me for the duration of the trial. He knew as much about me as anyone could know. He was not there to protect me from Al King; he was there to protect Al King from me!

After a few minutes we heard the familiar words, "All rise!" The tension began to mount as the lawyers and court reporters entered along with Judge Moye. The gavel went down. All eyes were glued to the front entrance as Alvin Lee King walked into the courtroom.

Al King came in facing the audience. He was chained with leg shackles. His hands were cuffed and attached to a waist belt and crotch chain. All he could do was breathe and blink. King was turned to face the judge. Some words were quietly spoken, and they sat him down directly in front of me. No one separated me from him-only two empty wooden benches and a small rail. It was obvious that extreme security measures had been planned for, even in the courtroom itself.

After all these months of terrible agony, I saw in person for the first time the man who had murdered my daughter. I felt fear as I breathed heavily and as an unbelievable rage of emotions raced through my mind. All during this time a single thing remained at the forefront of my mind. "Keep in control! Don't do anything that could possibly jeopardize him staying in the courtroom!" I couldn't let any outburst of emotions be seen or heard that defense attorney Percy Foreman might use to get a change of venue consideration, which was what the media had already predicted.

I had actually come prepared to seek revenge in the most extreme manner. I had come to do the same thing to Al King that he had done to Gina. However, God intervened in such a gentle way. He put the powerful potential of death on one side of me, in the person of Texas Ranger Brantley Foster. He placed the greatest example of love on the other side of me, in the person of my mother.

My mother said very little. She was a grandmother who was there along with everyone else to see that justice was done. The Ranger said nothing. The competency hearing began, and I was glad to see it. We had made the right decision. It was better this way. Nevertheless, I HAD to be there. I knew I was sitting just several feet away from the literal personification of the deadliest evil I had ever sensed.

I knew that I was not in the presence of the schoolteacher at Daingerfield High School or the systems engineer for IBM or the holder of a PhD with grants from the National Science Foundation. These were the credentials that floated on the surface of Al King's activities, but I knew that I was in the presence of a KILLER! On the Monday following the shootings, this man was to have stood trial for the charges of incest filed by his daughter. He was a man raised in a home shared with a pawnshop, a liquor store, and childhood pets that included a lion, a cougar, and a baboon. He was a professed atheist who lived a life with dark, questionable involvements.

The normal legal comments were made by King's attorneys to try to prove that their client was not competent to stand trial and never would be. Foreman was trying to be as non-offensive as possible to the people of Morris County. This was his tactic, and his strategy was clear from the beginning. He brought to the courtroom an aura of fear. His reputation was without question as the people listened to his eloquence. His assistants were quick and sharp. He was one of the best, and it was obvious. Maybe he had something up his sleeve that no one knew. In reality people feared his capabilities more than anything else.

Al King never moved. His elbows rested on the arms of his chair while his hands were folded together in front of him. His feet were slightly bent under the chair as he sat motionless. Jim Stanley, the prosecutor, did not seem at all shaken by the presence of Percy Foreman and his assistants. Stanley delivered his arguments with authority. He presented not only King's ability to stand trial but also his ability to do so in Morris County. Leon Jaowarski, United States Supreme Court prosecutor, had offered his assistance to Stanley. Stanley, however, felt confident that he could effectively represent the office of District Attorney.

Both Stanley and Foreman knew that the psychologist at John Sealy Hospital in Galveston had already ruled King competent. In reality, these proceedings were more of a legal charade than anything else, but they proceeded anyway. The time of waiting had allowed conjecture to build to the point of explosion. People were strained by the thought that if King were not ruled competent during this last hearing, he might not stand trial at all. This was Foreman's plan.

Foreman said that there was no doubt that King was guilty, but on the other hand there was no doubt that he was insane. His intent was to attempt to get the trial moved because of all the media coverage and prejudice in the community against his client.

Stanley's response to this argument was simple. He said that if that were so, then the trial would have to be moved out of the United States!

Judge Moye declared that there would be no change in location and that a jury could be selected on the court's ruling for competency.

Scores of people paraded by the District Attorney and testified as to the bizarre activities of Al King. Even during this time, I never took my eyes off of him. The actual proceedings had become vague to me, mainly due to the fact that I was concerned with only two things. I wanted the law to find him guilty and render a just verdict—death. If the law couldn't do it or wouldn't do it, I was fully prepared to do it myself.

Finally, sometime between 10:00 and 11:00 a.m. the district attorney called Texas Ranger Brantley Foster to the stand. Foster played the tape from the Sunday morning service on June 22. This tape, which had been in the custody of the Texas Rangers, was the bomb that the prosecutor had been waiting for to orchestrate his plan. Stanley had had enough of Foreman's cat-and-mouse game.

The surviving members of the victims' families listened solemnly. In addition to the tape there were sounds of muffled crying, and sorrow permeated the atmosphere of the courtroom. The tape was played only once and in its entirety. Even though the tape recorder was small, it could be heard clearly.

During this time my eyes were on Al King. If a man is truly insane, it is unusual for him to make any response. There would be no visible remorse or sign of care—only a vacant stare. Instead, Al King moved for the first time during the hearing. He became restless, dropped his head, and shuffled his feet.

The tension in the courtroom became volatile. Defense Attorney Percy Foreman must have felt it. He was representing the most hated man in Morris County that day. That made him the second most hated, and it was obvious. When the tape began to play, he simply sat down.

Even the judge noticed a change in the atmosphere. He dismissed the hearing until the next day. I watched King leave the courtroom surrounded by no less than eight to ten policemen. No one could even get close to him, but I tried.

I lunged forward, and tried to get King's attention over the noise of the crowd. "KING! KING!" I yelled as I moved through the crowd toward him. "LOOK AT ME! KING! LOOK IN MY FACE!"

Norman Crisp, pastor of First Baptist Church of Daingerfield, grabbed me by the arm, not knowing what I might try to do. "Larry," he said, "come on. This will do no good. Let's get out of here."

I continued to try to get King's attention. Then all of a sudden King turned and looked straight into my face. We made eye contact for a split second. That's all it took. Nothing else needed to be said. I followed Pastor Crisp and the Texas Rangers out of the courtroom.

I asked my mother if she was all right. Then I slipped by the media without one question and headed back to my home in Pittsburg, Texas. I felt like the tape had accomplished a blow that needed to be delivered. Once at home I nervously awaited the next day.

On the second day of the hearing, King was brought into the courtroom and seated in the same chair as the day before. I was again focused solely on him until Percy Foreman stood up and called the only character witness available for Alvin Lee King.

The character witness was a young man in his late teens or early twenties, dressed in bell bottom pants, elevator shoes, a pink shirt with a plaid sport coat, and wearing dark John Lennon type eyeglasses. He took the stand and was administered the oath. I fastened my eyes on him and thought, "What circus did they find this guy in?" He was tall and slender, dressed like a clown, and wore his hair in an Afro look. He began to answer Foreman's questions concerning his father's character.

I recalled what I had been told about the reason Al King was under indictment of a grand jury. He was under indictment for seventeen counts of incest from charges filed by his own daughter, who had moved to Houston to escape the abuse. King could not muster one character witness on his behalf, which was needed to give evidence that he was a good man. And he was a wife beater. His wife, a teacher in the Daingerfield school system, had come to work several times wearing sunshades to hide black eyes. King had been reported to the school administration for driving a school bus with children on board into people's yards. He was trying to run over a dog that was chasing the bus—all the while yelling obscenities at the animal.

Now on the witness stand sat a young man ready to be the only character witness for the most hated man in Morris County. After the oath was given, Percy Foreman stepped up and asked the question, "Would you please tell the court how you feel about your friend, Al King?"

The young man responded, "My friend is a good man, a good father, and one who cares about his family. He has provided for them well." The statement gave the impression of being well coached and well rehearsed. It was the most obvious lie that could ever have been given about a man who, it was rumored, had legally disowned some of his own family!

I thought how deceived this young man had become to give such nice attributes to this horrible creature. Sure he was a father, but the facts were speaking louder than his words.

The attorney for Al King asked one more question. "Would you tell the court how you feel about what your friend is accused of?"

He replied, "Whatever my friend started, I can finish!"

The statement was, to say the least, explosive! I could hear the groans and gasps coming from all over the courtroom. The comments that were being made from the gallery grew louder by the second.

Judge Moye slammed the gavel, called for order and quiet and then promptly called for a recess and for the attorneys to go to his chambers. Things were getting pretty rowdy in this East Texas courtroom. Several officers had made moves to get around this guy because of the crowd's angry comments made in response to this statement.

I shifted my focus from Al King to his friend because if this was King's friend then he was my enemy. Six officers quickly removed Al King toward the same door he had come through earlier while his friend was escorted out a side door of the courtroom. The crowd of people was beginning to sound like an Old West lynch mob. These piney woods folks had become like a well-disturbed hornets' nest.

I moved across the aisle toward the main lobby. As I rounded the corner of the lobby, I came face to face with the friend of Al King. I was so shocked that I came to a sudden stop in a frozen stance. Our eyes met with coldness and the anger of raging bulls.

I immediately reacted saying, "My name is Larry Linam," as I backed him against the wall by grabbing his coat. "I am the father of the seven-year-old girl whom your friend killed and if you want to finish what he started, how about starting with me—right now!"

I was in no mood to make an idle threat. My first blow hit the mark, followed by several crushing others that sent Al King's friend to the floor in a semi-conscious state. The whole time I was unleashing my fury upon this man, four policemen were trying to get us separated, but I managed somehow to move around them to complete the process.

Two of the law officers moved me quickly down the hall toward the side doors and then outside. After things calmed down, they strongly encouraged me to leave. I did! After all, I knew that if they wanted me, I would be the easiest man in town to find. I was not hiding anything or hiding from anyone.

Al King's friend managed to get back to one of the defense attorneys and asked if anything could be done to me for beating him. The attorney replied, "In any other county in the state of Texas you could prosecute Mr. Linam for this hit, but at the present time and under these circumstances and in Morris County, you can forget it!"

It was reported to me that Al King's friend made a visit that night to Al King and told him, "Look what has happened to me! The father of the seven-year-old girl did this to me!" Al King made no response at that time. However, sometime between 10:00 p.m. and 2:00 a.m. Al King ended the whole thing by hanging himself with cloth strips torn from a towel in his cell.

The next morning as I sat at my desk finishing some reports, my plant supervisor came in and said, "Larry, have you heard any news broadcasts on the radio yet?"

"No," I replied. "What's up?"

"You need to call Jim Stanley at the courthouse in Daingerfield. He has been trying to reach you and here is his phone number."

I called and identified myself. Immediately Mr. Stanley came on the line and said, "Larry, I wanted you to hear it from me about Al King—he's dead."

I thanked him and hung up. I just sat there in a daze.

My plant superintendent, asked if I needed to go home for the day. If I did, he could cover for me. I declined to take the whole day but took some time out when a close friend came up to the office. As I talked to him, I said, "I know this seems cold, but I feel as though I have been cheated out of justice. I wanted to see this man die before my very eyes."

I realized that by suicide Al King was still dead, and Al King was, as far as I was concerned, where he deserved to be. For me, however, it was the beginning of many years of suppressed anger and torment. My life was becoming a nightmare of unmitigated proportions. I have traveled through many valleys and many dark times, but I have reconciled, recovered, and even reclaimed good relationships.

CHAPTER 7 – DEVASTATED BY DIVORCE

How the world can change in just a short length of time! My memory goes back to the day when I felt the constant tugging at my heart to return to the calling to which the Lord led me at the age of seventeen. I was realizing that God's call on my life had never left me; I had left it. The desire to preach the gospel message and lead people into a life of peace and joy found in Jesus Christ as Lord had been the most fulfilling experiences of my life. However, the struggles of coping with life had become constant and arduous for me. I wanted to be around people again so that I could get to know and become a vital part of the community.

The memory of traveling across this great land of ours while sharing a story of how the Lord helped me through some of the most horrible days of tragedy that a person could experience was always fresh on my mind. I cannot count how many times I had been part of an event where the program to be presented consisted of professional gospel and country Western music artists. I guess one could say that it put me in with a group of some sort of celebrity status, but the truth is I did not feel like a part of that grouping. The story I had to tell was so filled with tragedy and horror but ended with some of the greatest victories a person could experience. That is what the people needed and wanted to hear.

I remember a conversation with a good friend of mine. "I would really like to get back to the work which was meant for me to do in life. I need to get back into a full-time ministry as a pastor of a church." As I conveyed this to my friend who had known me all my adult life, I saw a look of concern come over his face. He had seen the trials of the ministry on this level himself and he knew that the challenges could be hard to meet if I had to come from a comfort zone. I had truly been in that realm of a comfort zone for the past three years and this would be totally different.

One day the phone rang and as I answered I recognized the voice of my friend. I asked, "To what do I owe the honor of this call?" I figured that it was the time for another one of those fishing trips so that we could come back and tell about the big one that got away.

He said, "Larry, I just got off the phone with a friend of mine out in west Texas and the church he attends is looking for a pastor. The church would be full-time and has a staff in place. Would you mind if I sent your resumé to them?"

I told him that it would be fine, but I would like to revise it somewhat before doing so and that I would get it done and send it to him in a day or two.

After a few weeks the phone rang and the voice on the other end identified himself as the chairman of the pastor search committee for the East Cisco Baptist Church, Cisco, Texas. After exchanging the normal cordialities, he informed me that the committee had viewed my resume several times and would like to come to hear me preach and discuss with me the possibility of my becoming the pastor of their church. To which I responded, "I would like that very much."

So the arrangements were made and the committee came, I preached, and then we all went to dinner at a local diner in Paris, Texas. The end result of the dinner meeting was an invitation to come and preach in view of a call. That's what church folk call it when a person is asked to preach his best message and then they all take a vote on you and if you get the thumbs up, you're in! Well, I got the thumbs up, and I was in!

Then I accepted the call to pastor the East Cisco Baptist Church in Cisco, Texas, a church comprised mostly of people in their late fifties and sixties. God had other things in mind for that church, the city of Cisco, and for me. I had prayed, "Oh, God, let me be somewhere that you can use my life and experiences to affect an entire city for your glory and somewhere that individuals and families alike can begin to find or renew a powerful relationship with you." This is exactly what God had in mind for Cisco and for the East Cisco Baptist Church. Some would classify this church as a spiritual graveyard and an organization just going through the motions of being religious. Life can be that way too, for a lot of people; for after all, a church is made up of people.

Immediately God began to move in my heart and mind. I did not want to find myself in an office as the administrator of an organization, but on the streets as the evangelist of the city. I left the confines of the church office by instructing the church secretary, "If I get calls from the members, please take their names and numbers so I can call them back. I'll check in every hour or so." Door after door and house after house, I met people who were looking for answers to questions that had been left unanswered by the things of the world. I had the answer that brought peace and results for lives of many: faith and salvation in Jesus Christ.

Day after day and Sunday after Sunday, I preached with the fervency and zeal of an evangelist. My sixteen-year-old son, Jeff, my thirteen-year-old daughter, Jennifer, and my seventeen-year-old foster son Johnny encouraged their friends to become a part of something good and wholesome by coming to church with them. The effect of these three young people was making a big difference in the life of the church and people in their fifties and sixties soon found themselves a church of young couples and youth. There were new faces of all ages. The congregation swelled from ninety 90 or so to 200 or more on Sunday mornings. People were smiling with eyes of joy and amazement. There were hugs and happy reunions.

All this did not just happen overnight. It had taken three years of diligent work, much prayer, and a dedication to the Scriptures. The most important thing of all was being a good example before the people as I walked and talked among them. The growth and strength of the church was remarkable, but in my heart and mind there was a new nightmare. I found myself buried in the ongoing demands of the ministry and the needs of new converts to know more about the Lord and what the Bible teaches about living the Christian life. I had only a handful of trained people in the church to help nurture their minds and hearts and to meet the needs of many. I worked with the new members in discipleship training, while another member took the youth class, which had grown from five to seventy-five.

The problems that arise from such growth come in various sizes and shapes and sometimes in multiple numbers. I began to experience all of these along with specific problems with personnel. It had come to my attention that there seemed to be more emphasis on pizza, cookies, cokes, and parties than on biblical teaching. So, being the leader and person responsible for the educational program in the church, I addressed the issue with all those concerned with the task. I was not prepared for the response that was generated. The division among the staff grew at an alarming speed and the gap between us became larger than the Grand Canyon. I was buried in other affairs of the church and now this! Church members, those so-called watchdogs of the Lord's house, sometimes can be very vicious. Their bark and bite can hurt the heart and soul of dedicated servants and sometimes even halt the work of the Holy Spirit.

I had become so embroiled in the handling of the problems of the church that I had not noticed the effect all this was having on my personal life. I had become isolated even from my family. One Sunday morning I was ready to go to the office (I always went early on Sunday) and I noticed the other family members were kind of dragging things out. But I went on anyway, thinking they will catch up later. I wondered what was wrong but did not ask. I just went out the door and made my way to the church for another Sunday of preaching and pastoral responsibilities.

The events that were about to unfold were of such devastating proportions that I could in no way have conceived the magnitude of them. As a pastor of a church that had experienced such tremendous growth and with a ministry that had a very positive influence on the community, I should have been "sitting on top of the world." The Sunday morning service was about to begin when, as I headed up the steps to the pulpit platform, all of a sudden, a huge sensation of nausea came over me. In my twenty-four years of ministry, I had never been sick even one Sunday, but all of a sudden I felt like my insides were about to come out of me.

I looked out over the congregation and saw our director of missions who was a retired pastor. Knowing that most retired pastors have one of those "old standby" messages that can be delivered "at the drop of a hat," I appealed to him. "Brother, I know this is highly irregular but could you come to the pulpit and bring the morning message for me? I am feeling so ill that I must go home." He consented without hesitation to bring the message. I apologized to the congregation and excused myself, got to my car, and began to drive toward the house. As I drove home, I was thinking, "Lord, why am I feeling so terrible on the day that I literally live to see from week to week? I witness everyday to see people trust you as Lord of their lives and to come make their profession of faith in you. Now, on the day that is so significant in the week, I feel like I am wasted and totally useless."

The answer was about to come!!!!

Getting out of the car and heading into the house, I noticed that none of the other vehicles were in the drive. I thought OK, they are all at church. The untruth of that statement was about to hit me full bore. I reached for the doorknob and opened the door. Then I went through the doorway and pushed the door shut, thinking, "I am about to throw up!" All of a sudden the most deafening sound, the most alarming sound I have ever heard echoed throughout the house. "Slam-Slam-Slam!" as the door slammed shut, its echoes resounded from wall to wall from room to room.

No one was there. The furniture was gone. There was no couch, no TV, no kitchen table, nothing! The thought of the illness that had come on me all of a sudden was overridden by the overwhelming sense of nothingness. Abandonment! It was the worst fear that a minister of the gospel could feel. This was not supposed to happen. I felt the horror of losing the most precious thing that I valued the most, what I had worked to provide for, but that was now non existent in the house. It was no longer the nausea that plagued me, but the horrible feeling that my heart was breaking in two, crushing my physical being.

It was at this point that I began to do the only thing I knew to do, which was to pray. "God, please help me understand what is happening," I prayed as I went from room to room in a house that was under the strong attack of Satan with what seemed to be a legion of demons oppressing me at every turn. One must realize that just as there is a heaven and a hell, there are angels and there are demons, the fallen angels since before the creation of the world. Here stood a man in the midst of defiance, deception, and what was later to become a divorce,

Satan is a mastermind at the process of undermining the structure of the home as God intended it to be. The Apostle Paul gives us the formula for the home in Ephesians 5:22-23 which says: *"Wives, submit to your own husbands, as to the Lord. For the husband is head of the wife, as also Christ is head of the church; and He is the Savior of the body. Therefore, just as the church is subject to Christ, so let the wives be to their own husbands in everything. Husbands, love your wives, just as Christ also loved the church and gave himself for it, that He might sanctify and cleanse it with the washing of water by the word, that He might present it to Himself a glorious church, not having spot or wrinkle or any such thing, but that it should be holy and without blemish. So husbands ought to love their own wives as their own bodies; he who loves his wife loves himself. For no one ever hated his own flesh, but nourishes and cherishes it, just as the Lord does the church. For we are members of His body, of His flesh and of His bones. For this reason a man shall leave his father and mother and be joined to his wife, and the two shall become one flesh. This is a great mystery, but I speak concerning Christ and the church. Nevertheless let each one of you in particular so love his own wife as himself, and let the wife see that she respects her husband."* The husband is to be the head of the home and the wife is to be in submission to the husband. Please do not interpret this to mean that the husband is to rule with a fist of iron. The husband is responsible for and to the family as a whole. His position is to bring godly elements of love, provision, and guidance into the home for the sake of the family. This also is supported by what the apostle Paul says in Ephesians 6: 1-4: "*Children obey your parents in the Lord, for this is right. Honor your father and mother, which is the first commandment with promise: that it may be well with you and you may live long on the earth. And you, fathers, do not provoke your children to wrath, but bring them up in the training and admonition of the Lord.*"

I had lived my faith in front of my family. Jeff had won the trust and admiration of his peer group. Johnny had helped Jeff witness to the football team members about the meaning of salvation in Jesus Christ. Why were they able to do this? Maybe it was because these young men had seen me lead many individuals to faith in the Lord. Many times children had brought friends to me at home or at church to have me explain the biblical plan of salvation. Because of that, should I not have their reverence and respect as a father and among the family?

I was not ready to give up on a twenty-four-year marriage and relationship even if it had "gone south," as they say when things start going bad and sour. The process of reconciliation is not an easy thing to do when the spirit of a person is hurting and suffering from the type of shock that had been given to me but I wanted to try to make whatever changes needed to be made, so long as the changes were reasonable and equitable. I really thought that all problems had solutions and that would be true if marriage was nothing more than math problems.

I could not imagine what all the problems were that would lead to such a huge gap in my family relationship but the reality was telling me that there were some real breakdowns in communication among us. I knew that I needed some help in coming to a good level of understanding and the one person I knew that could bring all this in perspective was the counselor who had helped me to understand the realities of the traumatic loss of our daughter.

The rolodex on the counter would hold the information to make the contact to the one person I felt could bring some understanding to my troubled mind. I picked out the card with the telephone number and made the call.

The voice on the other end of the line said, "Family counseling. May I help you."

I said, "This is Larry Linam, and I would like to speak to Dr. Thomas if possible."

"Why, Larry, it is good to hear from you after all these years. This is Shirley, and I remember you well. Dr. Thomas was just at my desk and is in his office; let me ring him for you."

Dr. Thomas answered, "Larry, great to hear your voice. How are things going out in west Texas?"

I responded, "Not so good, it seems that after ten years I have hit a problem that I am not sure how to deal with it and was wondering if you would have time to help me understand a few things and help me find some answers to some issues because I am not sure my thinking abilities are what they should be right now."

The reply was quick and decisive, "Sure. When would you like to come to Tyler? I have some time this week, or next week I have several openings every day."

I thought about getting permission to be off the church field for several days. I would need to find suitable pulpit supply and I would also need to arrange for all the things necessary to fill the responsibilities that a pastor has to do when being out of town for more than a few days.

"Dr. Thomas, I feel like I am going to need some extensive counseling and maybe some evaluation work. So, if possible let's set up a couple of hours a day for three or four days next week beginning on Monday."

He said, "Larry, I am penciling it into my schedule right now. The sound of your voice and decision to come for this length of time tells me that you are facing some big problems in the marriage. Is this a correct assessment of thinking?"

"Yes, sir," I responded.

"OK, I will see you on Monday, 10 a.m. And Larry, I will begin praying for you as you come. We will find some answers when you get here. I want you to think about taking a full battery of personal evaluation tests. It will take a week to do it."

I knew that these comments were right on target as Dr. Thomas always is, so I replied, "Sounds good to me. I will make arrangements to be in Tyler the entire week."

I made my plans, informed all concerned parties of the family and then made a call to my cousin who happened to live in Tyler. He owned a beautiful lake house on Lake Palestine just out of Tyler. Everything seemed to be set except for my own mind and unending questions that lingered within me.

The trip to Tyler began early the following Monday morning with a prayer as I pulled out of the drive and made my way to the interstate highway which would take me directly to where I would find out if there was deep emotional problems within me. I had heard that when a marriage begins to have difficulty that it results from a combination of things such as finances, broken-down communication, or past traumatic experiences. I had begun to see some of these tendencies while realizing that the last of the three could be a very strong possibility. I just kept asking myself, "What could have all of a sudden happened to bring me to this point when traumatic loss was ten years past?" The drive to Tyler was either shorter than anticipated or my prayer was longer than I had thought because as I looked a couple of hundred yards down the interstate the sign read that Tyler is the next four exits. In a matter of minutes I was sitting in the parking lot of my friend and counselor's clinic.

I walked into the receptionist area and a voice said, "You must be Larry."

To which I responded, "Yes, I am. Is Dr. Thomas in?" And just about the time I finished the question, Dr. Thomas stepped out of the coffee room and asked if my trip was OK and would I like a cup of coffee. I was ready for the coffee and the meeting with Dr. Thomas. He has a very easy mannerism and warm spirit when dealing with people and can make a person feel as if he is his entire focus in life. I knew that God had put me in the right place at the right time. I had prayed all the way to Tyler that God would give me the courage to accept whatever was to come my way. If Larry Linam was the sole element of the problem, then I needed to face whatever it is that had to be addressed and make the necessary adjustments to bring about reconciliation with biblical and spiritual results.

Dr. Thomas began with a direct approach with a real good question, "Larry, tell me where you think the problems began. In other words, let's start at the beginning."

I must have been more focused than I imagined because for the next forty-five minutes I spoke my every thought without stopping as he sat and made several pages of notes. It was like a volcano erupting and the magma was flowing down the sides. The words were just spilling out of me! I was ready to talk and Dr. Thomas was more than willing to listen.

The session ended with Dr. Thomas telling me that we needed to get started in the morning with some testing which would help establish the full evaluation process and tell us basically if I was insane or what. I sure hoped and prayed for the "what."

Tuesday morning we began the testing which lasted for three days. Some of the many questions were multiple choice and others were true/false. I was also given a set of questions to take home with me or should I say to the lake house, to give composition type answers. I was beginning to think that by the end of the week I would really be close to insanity or find some real good solutions to all my problems. However, about the end of the third day Dr. Thomas made a suggestion that I stay an additional week with him. I thought, "O, Lord, am I really this bad off? Am I headed for a total breakdown of massive destruction in life?"

Immediately Dr. Thomas reassured me, "Larry, some of the indicators on the battery of tests you have completed are showing us what we call 'positive indicators' which simply means we know what tack to take and I am preparing an in-depth plan of guidance suggestions for you."

I said, "You mean I am not going to die or be cast into prison?"

He said, "I think you will like what I have for you, considering the severity of your circumstances."

So I made a few phone calls to let people back in Cisco know what was taking place. I wanted them to know that everything seemed to be going fine. I also wanted to see if any problem there would prevent me from staying another week in Tyler. So for the next week Dr. Thomas and I worked together until the Thursday of the second week. He came into this office as I sat in the corner looking out the window, and said, "Larry, I have all your test scores and evaluations on your answers. Would you like to look at them with me?"

I replied, "Well doc, I guess this is what these last two weeks have been about. Let's see if Larry Linam is normal or crazy."

Page by page Dr. Thomas went over the results with me until we came to the last page. He just looked at me with an expression of genuine concern and said, "Larry, the last page is a chart consisting of three different shaded levels. The first level is "abnormal," the second is "normal," and the third or bottom level is "subnormal." With that explanation he removed the last page, which was turned with the blank side up and placed it in my hand.

As I turned the sheet over, I looked at the single red line drawn on the sheet and gasped a huge sigh of relief! I was NORMAL!!!! I had been thinking that maybe some folks that thought I was crazy were right. But this was great news to me. The past two weeks became worth all the effort and time spent missing folks that I loved dearly and being away from all the struggles back home. Now I felt like I could get a grip on moving toward a level of reconciliation and problem resolution with some degree of understanding. I had some hope returning to my life that had not been there before.

Dr. Thomas looked at me with a smile and began to tell me that he had made some phone calls to the references I had listed in our first session. I had given him permission to contact them for the purpose of getting full disclosure. He explained to me that not everyone felt good about the reconciliation process as I did. My heart sank to the floor and as I looked at him, I knew what that meant.

I said, "What do you think I need to do at this point and time?"

Dr. Thomas replied, "Larry, I have known you for over ten years and I know that a lot of things change in those years. No one stays the same, and when traumatic events come along sometimes the results of those things have delayed effects on us. What I am saying is that the best I can gather from all of you and I have shared these past two weeks and the information that I have been able to gather, I feel that you need to get a good attorney because your marriage is over."

I just slumped into the chair, and put my hands over my face for a few seconds. After that, I looked him in the eye as I had done many times before and said, "Know what, Doc? I think you hit the nail on the head. Just down the street from your office, my cousin is an attorney and I need to have a talk with him."

The reality of the effects of anger, bitterness, argument, and terrible communication had shown its ugly side. The pressures of conflict and unforgiving spirits and attitudes had taken seed and were now bringing a harvest of awful proportion. The attack of Satan on my life was pronouncing itself with "a man devastated by divorce."

I had made my way back to Cisco with this news and a short-lived glimmer of hope. I arrived back at the house; for it was no longer a home. I went to the chair in the corner of the bedroom and sat down. I stayed in that chair in the dark corner in that room for two weeks in a state of personal depravity. I had no one to speak to, no one to love or to love me. During those seventeen days of darkness, silence, and loneliness, I had nothing to eat, drink, or say. I was the ultimate figure of isolation and desolation. I was feeling what seemed to be a living death, which I came to know as "divorce."

Chapter 8 – Out of the Darkness— Into the Light

Depression, the darkness that over-whelmed me, was such a debilitating feeling that it literally affected me from the inside out. I had served the lord with strength, tenacity, and complete faith. I had sought to be the kind of pastor whom any church would be proud to have lead the church. Now I sat alone in a dark room. I was a man who had cared for others, but now it seemed that no one cared about me. I had answered the phone at all hours to listen to someone who was crying in the night. I thought nothing of getting out of bed, getting dressed, and driving hundreds of miles to be with a grieving family and to console them in the loss of a loved one. Now, not a single call came day or night to listen or to console me.

I did not know that hundreds of miles away my parents were petitioning the Lord in prayer that He would be with their son. I did not see the man watching outside my window, looking in to see if I was still in the chair and doing OK for the time being. The man outside was deeply interested in me, but he did not want to call out or disturb me.

One day I was startled by a knock on the door, a sound I had not heard in quite some time. I answered the door, looking literally like a bum. I had not shaved, eaten, or gotten out of the chair except to go to the bathroom. I opened the door wide enough to see a man standing on the front porch. "Larry," the man said, "you don't know me, but my pastor, John Jones, told us that we need to be praying for you during this time in your life. He asked me to please come by each day to check with you to see if there might be anything that folks at Mountain Top Church could do for you."

I just stood there not knowing what to say or do, but I finally invited the man in, learned his identity, and thanked him for coming by. The man prayed with me and reassured me that I would be on the hearts and minds of the church each time they met. In my emotional state, even this act of kindness, someone simply coming by, began to be more than I could handle. I had felt that life and all its goodness had left me over the previous fifteen days. The fact that someone came by sent stabs of pain, sorrow, and anger through my heart and soul, and the chair once again became my refuge. For fifteen days, I had done nothing except weep my heart away in the darkness. Now new emotions were taking over as I began to express my hurt, my anger, and my pain that had been sealed inside.

At dawn on the sixteenth day of my self-imposed isolation, I was still sitting in my chair. I did not know or even care that night had come and gone. I had not moved except that I did notice the silhouette just outside the window of the dark room where I sat. Whether I realized it or not, many concerned people were beginning to ask questions about their pastor and their friend. The man in the shadows could have answered the questions.

The man outside my window was not a window peeper. He was, in fact, the best friend I could have had at this time. A. J. Booth, a deacon at East Cisco Baptist Church, finally decided to knock at my door that morning. After I answered the door and invited A. J. to come inside, he sat down across from me. "Larry," A. J. said, "your mom and dad have been calling me every day to check on you because you told them days ago that you wanted to be alone. They sure are worried about you."

I looked up at A. J. and replied, "I know that they have been really concerned, but I just do not know what to say to them. I feel as though I have failed everyone who meant anything in my life."

"Larry," A. J. said, "You sure have lost some weight since I last saw you. Billie has fixed something for you to eat and has told me to stay here and visit with you while you eat it." Billie, A. J.'s wife, was an excellent cook; and I had eaten meals with them many times. A. J. and I had become very close as friends and as Christians.

"Well," I said, "the food certainly does smell good; and I know that if Billie cooked it, it has to be really good." I got up, went into the kitchen to get eating utensils, and came back to the chair, which except for a bed and a freezer was about all the furniture I had left since the family moved out.

I looked around the room to see if there was another chair so I could offer A. J. a place to sit. The bed across the room had not been disturbed for over two weeks and did not even have a wrinkle in the bedspread. Looking at the bed I said to A. J., "I tell you what I'll do. For this time being, I'll sit on the bed and eat this food; and you can sit in the chair and visit with me for a while. OK?"

The time seemed to just fly by as the food quickly disappeared. I looked at my friend who was sitting in the chair, and I began to try to make some excuse for getting back into the corner and back into the darkness. Instead, something different began to take place. I realized that it had been two weeks since I had left that chair for more than five minutes at a time. That chair had been home to me far too long.

Turning to A. J., I asked, "Do you know what I'd like to do?"

A. J. responded, "No, what?"

"I'd like to go take a shower and shave, I think it might make me feel a little refreshed and relax me some. I don't know why, but I feel exhausted; yet I know that I have just sat in a chair and done absolutely nothing." Weak and tired, I said good-bye to my friend and then made my way to the back of the house.

As I made my way down the hallway, I came to what used to be Jennifer's room, and I shut the door. Then I went on to what used to be Jeff's room, and once again I just shut the door. Why not? No one lived in there anymore. It was then that I remembered the words my children spoke to me, "Dad, we love you just as much as mom, and we intend to spend as much time with you as with mom."

I didn't quite believe that statement because it had become very clear that the kids had made a deal. The children were to have total freedom to do what they wanted and to go where they wanted so long as they did not live with me. Now, if you were a teenager and someone told you that you could have complete freedom and no accountability process, what would you choose to do? The end result, as far as I was concerned, was that I had not seen or heard from either of my children in months.

I asked myself many times every day, "I wonder if they care if I'm dead or alive? Would they come to the funeral if I died?" These questions sounded as though a real pity party was taking place. The fact was that I was so emotionally exhausted and physically drained that I could not be anything but negative. This is how Satan brings a person to the point of total disparity. Even in the life of a Christian that has served God's plan and purpose, the devil will rob the joy and peace that God gives. My spirit was defeated, and my desire to do God's will was defeated in every way possible.

As I entered the bathroom, tired and weak, I looked over in the corner and at the scales. I said aloud to myself, "Well, I guess there is one thing left that I can use." Stepping up on the scales, I discovered, much to my surprise, that I had lost thirty-seven pounds. This was hard to believe because I had tried to lose weight in the past, and it was always a battle, to say the least. All I could think of was, "What a way to lose weight! All I have to do to lose weight is lose my entire family without being able to see their faces or hear their voices."

The irony of all this is that the kids had lived only blocks from me for the past ten months prior to the divorce. I remembered that just after they had left and moved into the apartment in Cisco, I could stand, looking out the bathroom window, and see the lights on the apartment where my family lived without me.

I could do nothing better than to focus on all the negatives in my life and to see nothing positive. I was defeated, disillusioned, but worst of all, divorced. I felt the pain of all that was missing from my life. The family that I had cared for and loved with an undying faithfulness was now just something that, in reality, existed only in my mind.

I stood there thinking to myself, "Lord, I have chosen to be true and faithful to what You have called me to do. It seems as though everything around me is in total ruin, and I cannot figure out why. I need some kind of indication that I have made the right decision in staying with my commitment to the calling You placed in my life."

I looked out the window one last time and decided that what might really feel good at this time would be a nice hot shower and maybe a walk outside the house for a little while.

The next five days were going to be an experience I would never forget because of the extreme emotional upheaval that would take place in my life. The strangeness of the experience was that I would travel to the neighboring city of Abilene, a city only sixty miles away; yet it would take me five days to get there.

Going out to eat among other people seemed like a good idea, but as the old saying goes, "It's easier said than done." The car had not moved out of the garage in over two weeks. I backed down the drive and followed the route to the interstate, which would take me to Abilene. Immediately I began to feel the awesome weight of being alone in the car with no one to talk to and no one to share the drive down the highway.

Two miles down the interstate I began to experience the feeling of desolation. My tears began to flow like streams of water down a hillside after a good rain, making it difficult to see to drive. I pulled the car over to the side of the road, hoping that no one would come by and recognize me.

"Oh, Lord," I cried, "I cannot go on like this, I need some help. I cannot even get two miles down the road to go eat. How am I going to face each day feeling like as though no one cares enough to be with me?"

I felt the full weight of the recent events crushing me beneath the sense of extreme failure, the failure of the marriage and the family, and now the failure to travel just sixty miles to go to a restaurant to eat. Having gone only two miles down the interstate, I turned the car around, crossed the median, and began driving back to the house. Back at the house, I found myself back in the chair that had been home to me for the past weeks.

During the drive I had cried so much that the pressure of my swollen eyes made me want to fall asleep. Before drifting off after I returned to the house, I muttered these words, "Lord, I have no one to talk with but You. I'm not expecting a visible or audible expression from You right now, but I would like to just have a little rest to refresh my tired, weary mind and body." With those words of desperation, I seemed to fall right off to sleep as soon as I got home.

The darkness of the first day was now history. The first day of a realization that I was no longer a family man, no longer a husband, nor did I possess the characteristics of being a guiding and loving father of two wonderful children and a fine foster child. I did not know that just driving down the road to get a break from the desolation of being alone in an empty and dark house was actually going to bring me closer to realizing that life was not over but just in a time of reformation.

I awoke from a night's rest, realizing that I had not even bothered to take my dress clothes off or put on my sleepwear. The truth of this is that it did not make any difference. This was the day after the big attempt to get out of the darkness, which had brought what appeared to be failure, just one more time.

I got to my knees to pray, "Lord, I know You are always there to hear the prayers of those who trust in You and believe in You. I am so tired of the loneliness and the personal darkness that seems to be all around me. Help me make it to Abilene and help me to feel that life has some kind of purpose and meaning for my being on this earth."

The dawning of the second day brought me out of bed and into the chair in the corner of the dark room, which I had called home. The prayer had seemed to help me step back and look at the situation as one that I could come to grips with.   After all, the only thing worse than this was death itself.

Out of the chair and into the shower again, I found myself on my way back to the interstate headed toward Abilene. Yes, I made another attempt to make it out of town. Just ahead of me on the right, I approached the three-mile mark and the Roadside Park and rest area just out of Cisco.

"I wish I could just see them one more time; oh, to hear their voices speaking any words at all." I spoke with a breaking voice. The tears were once again flowing like a river, and I made a quick exit from the interstate into the rest area. With my head down below the window level of the car and hoping that no one would see me, I began to brush the tears away as quickly as they came. The result was obvious. I simply moved my car toward the service road that would lead me back to the empty house to a chair that sat in a corner with no light around me.

The second day had done nothing except move me just one more mile down the road. "Larry, you are a fool for letting this situation destroy you when everyone in your family seems to be able to just go right on with life!" I chided myself.

Nonetheless I was in the chair, and the rest of the day would just pass me by as if life in the world did not need or want me for anyone or anything. What I did not feel was the release of just one more mile down the road and one more day of life in which God had not forsaken me but had been right there just as if I had asked. The second day was now history and would probably be forgotten if I had anything to do with it.

On the third day several people in the church called to ask me about my well-being. This should have made me feel really good, that someone would call just to check on me. I heard a knock on the door and there stood A. J., my best friend.

"Come on in A. J. I could sure use some company about this time." I spoke with a different tone of voice.

A. J. looked at me and said, "I know that you don't feel like being around people all that much, but I think it would sure do you some good to just get out of the house and maybe go to Abilene to the mall or out to eat."

I replied, "A. J., I have tried to go to Abilene the past two days and have not been able to get past the rest area just out of Cisco."

"Well, keep trying, at least you're getting closer to the goal, which is getting to Abilene," A. J. replied.

The little bit of encouragement that had been offered was more than just words from a friend. They seemed to be a message from the Lord, speaking to the side of me that was not dead, at least not yet. This was the competitive side that would not lay down to defeat or desolation. Little did I realize but the journey out of the darkness was about to lead me to the need to face the facts, rather than lament the lacks in my life.

The third day moved me toward the goal of traveling farther down the road in my attempt to go to Abilene; and that was done, in one sense of the word. I made it to the rest area, but I didn't stop in tears. This time it was different because I was feeling the anger of my situation. In fact, I became so angry in fact with what had befallen me that I went home and walked around the backyard, just thinking how Satan had been so successful at tearing my home apart and destroying another family as well as another ministry.

My anger was at the events of the past, not just the ministry, but the overwhelming tragedy of losing Gina at a point and time in life that was already difficult. The tragedy had come at a time when caring for and providing for three children and a wife had become no small task.

I had never been one to give up in defeat. I had worked as diligently and faithfully as I could, only to be segregated from my family and friend. Why? That one question plagued my very soul and mind.

"Lord, I asked You to allow me back into the ministry to serve You and to advance Your work. You did that, just as we agreed, and You have been faithful to me, as I have been to You. I am angry, alone, and feeling like a complete failure. Please answer this one question, why?"

I prayed this over and over into the late evening until exhaustion and sleep came to a weary and stressed body.

The fourth day began for me around 10:30 a.m. It was a real surprise to me that I could sleep until almost midday. The question of "why" still was fresh on my mind, as I drove down I-20 to Abilene, desiring to get out of Cisco for just a little while.

On this day prevailing anger built up in me, and I felt the pressure to the point of explosive frustration. By the time I really looked around me, I was in a small town just thirty miles from Abilene. The thought then hit me, "I can't be around anyone right now. I can't even respond to myself. I don't have any stability." I slammed my fist into the car seat beside me, leaving a deep impression on the seat's fabric. I turned the car around and returned to Cisco, returning to the safe haven I knew, the chair in the corner of a dark, empty room.

Sitting there in that desolation, the thought came to my mind, "Lord, I would rather be dead and with you than to suffer this terrible existence of life. I cannot get sixty miles down the highway to go out to eat. How am I going to be of any value to anyone?"

I had lost track of time because I had spent the fourth night of this journey sitting, thinking, and praying. I was a very pragmatic man, and I had never been one to say I heard voices; but today, the fifth day, I heard from God. After days of questioning, days of crying out to the only source of strength I knew, I heard something remarkable. In the silence of the early dawn, and as the rising sun lightened the sky, I heard in my corner of darkness an audible and understandable voice.

The voice said, "Larry, get up, get out, and go to Abilene."

I thought to myself, "That's not going to work. I have tried four days to go just sixty miles, four days of failure and frustration; but I'll be faithful. One more try, Lord. Just one more is all I can take!"

I moved as methodically as possible going through all the details of making myself presentable, should I actually succeed in getting to my favorite eating place in Abilene. Today the hours seemed to speed up, while in the previous days they had been long at certain times and just black at other times. I had quit thinking and had started following the directions of the voice I had heard, although it had not come from anything or anyone I had seen. To my surprise, on the fifth day I stood in the parking lot of my favorite Chinese restaurant in Abilene.

"I'll have the buffet, please," I managed to say to the waitress.

I remember how great the food tasted; and for the first time in months, a smile actually came across my face. I was really enjoying something; so I took my time, ate a lot of Chinese food, and then decided just to drive around the city. After all, it was a hot day in July. Not many folks were out in the heat, but I felt that the sunshine would be good for me. And it was!

Only one hour had passed, but driving around the city seemed to bring some welcome relief, some changes in the atmosphere. All of a sudden, something caught my attention as I approached a major intersection. On the corner of a parking lot was a small kiosk for something called Lemon Chill. The kiosk was colorful and sparked my curiosity.

I pulled into the parking lot and stepped out of the car and up to the order window. "What is Lemon Chill?" I asked.

The man at the window told me all about Lemon Chill and said, "Here, have a sample."

I tasted the sample of the lemon dessert and said, "Boy, this is really lemony; and it's really cold!"

"Yes, Sir," the man said. "Want one?"

"No, I'd like two of them, please." I spoke with a sense of anticipation.

I had been away from home nearly all day, and the time had flown by for me. The drive home was enjoyable because I had occupied myself with eating the newfound delight of Lemon Chill. I was a curious type, so I read all the information on the cup—calories, percentages, and ingredients. This stuff was really good!

I got home and put the second chill in my freezer. Then I sat down at the kitchen bar to finish the first one. Then I had a thought, "I'm supposedly an average guy with normal tastes; and if I like this enough to buy two at a time, it might be good to have some kiosks in this area." I looked at the small print on the lower section of the cup. The company had listed an 800 number. I picked up the phone and called the number.

A voice came on the line, "Lemon Chill, how may I help you?"

"My name is Larry Linam, and I'd like some information about ways that Lemon Chill is being marketed."

"Just a moment, I'll put you in touch with our marketing director. He can advise you," the lady said.

I got the information I needed, which sparked my interests even more. All of a sudden, it dawned on me that I had come home to the empty house, turned on the lights, sat down somewhere other than my dark corner, and had actually talked on the telephone to a live person. All this seemed new and refreshing to me as well, as providing a new process called self-analysis.

(By the way, I did go on to develop a strong and successful business with Lemon Chill.)

Sometimes it is good to reflect, but I had had nothing but denial and painful events for months. Now, however, I began to risk asking one very important question of myself in order to face my past.

As painful as reflection was for me, I now had a new thought in my mind after dwelling on all the denial and rejection that had come from the absence of being a father and a parent. You see, I had not even had the presence of my children in my house for some eight months. I had suffered the worst thing that a parent could be subjected to—rejection and disrespect. As I sat at the kitchen bar, I looked around my home at the few remains left, as evidence that I had once had a family.

With the new thought, a new light began to shine. I had other reasons to live and become productive in life, even in rejection. I wanted to live for my children, for my friends, and for my parents, especially my parents, the two people who had never once forsaken me.

I picked up the phone immediately.

"Hey, Mom, how are you?"

"Larry!" my mom cried as she spoke and my father listened on the other phone.

"Everything OK, Son?" my dad asked.

"Well, Dad, no, it's not, but it's going to get better. It can't get much worse now, could it?" I replied with a tone of dry wit, which is my communication nature or style.

After a few minutes of conversing with the two people who have never given up loving, praying, and caring for me, the outlook of life seemed much brighter.

"Mom, Dad, I don't know why I have waited so long to call you. I feel a lot better talking to you, because you both give me the assurance that nothing will separate us. I just could not imagine what others might think of this failure of mine," I said.

My dad replied, "Son, we, your mom and I, will always be here for you; and we realize that life does not always turn out the way we plan it."

"But, Larry, you must remember this always, while you have some responsibility in the marriage and its decline, you did not have all of the responsibility—it's a group effort," said my mother.

I replied, "I realize that I may have worked too hard or too much at trying to meet the demands on my time, but nonetheless I'm deciding to go on now. I just don't know exactly where yet. At least I can see Jeff when he plays football and runs track and Jennifer when she has a band event or recital performance." As the conversation ended, I began to find myself thinking that the responsibilities of my father status had not changed and that no form of separation while I am alive will change that.

The days turned to weeks and weeks into months. I had come to terms with the awful experience of divorce. I had realized that I had a right and privilege to be a father that I could still be an example to my children. The choices and decisions that I had to make needed to demonstrate soundness in life so those who desired positive results could achieve them.

There was still purpose and meaning in the years that lay ahead of me. I realized that in God's eyes I was still the same man whom he called at the age of seventeen. It did not matter what anyone thought. It only mattered that I cared about what God was receiving from me by way of obedience and faithfulness. The truth is, it was time to come out of the darkness and into the light!

Chapter 9 – The Experience of a Lifetime

I have discovered that when one decides to come into the light, one can start to see things from a different perspective. The darkness prevented me from seeing, thinking about, and understanding the obvious truths of God's Word and His will for my life. The changes that had occurred in my life were undeniably a "really bad experience." However, I was also realizing the truth of that old saying, "When life hands you a whole bunch of lemons, make some lemonade!"

The light I am thinking and writing about and now living is the wonderful process that only our Lord and Savior Jesus Christ can bring. The decision "to come to the light" was one that began the healing of the mortal wounds of a family death, the healing of the torn marriage, the redemption of a spiritual warrior. You see I had come to realize that real healing sometimes has to take place from the inside out. God brings not just healing but real victory in living when we commit to living for His glory. My life is really His story and His will, with His purpose, and most importantly, His timing. I want you to remember this passage of Scripture from **1 Peter 5:6-7**. "*Humble yourselves therefore, under the* *mighty hand of God, that He may exalt you at the proper time, casting all your anxiety upon Him, because He cares for you."*

This is just one of three thousand promises given in God's Word, but I felt this one was and is for me. The important matter of this Scripture is really personalized in **1 Peter 5:8-10** because I found that God wanted me to experience that wonderful position of winning in life instead of losing. I had a coach who told me one day in a practice session, "Linam, just remember, 'Losers never win and winners never lose.'" I believe the coach was saying to me that even if I suffer defeat from time to time, I have gained—I have won—because I have played the game.

Satan had delivered on me some of life's most devastating blows, intending to knock me out of being the spiritual warrior that God had purposed and designed me to be. Please remember that these strong hits began in October 1977, with my fist in the face of God and continued until early 1998. If you do some math here, you will discover that it was for more than twenty years! Two decades!

Dear friend, Satan was not immediately scared off just because I had decided "to come into the light." The attacks continued, but now there was a difference. I had become stronger in my faith and in the use and practice of God's Word. All this time God was doing battle for me. Now, please get this down—I Peter 5:9. I was making great strides in Christ. I began to "resist" Satan's attack on my faith and began returning glory to God in Christ, who was perfecting me, confirming me, strengthening me, and establishing me!

I was no longer in some dark, desolate, depressing, or lonely room. I was not sunk deep into a chair or regression. I began claiming the victory in Jesus, as in I John 5:4. *For whatever is born of God overcomes the world; and this is the victory that has overcome the world—our faith.*

I was embarking on a journey, an experience of a lifetime that would prove to be the redemption of a spiritual warrior. I realized that I was just one of hopefully many spiritual warriors out there in the world. However, I knew that this was "born of God" and that victory, not defeat, was on its way.

I had come to realize that making my way back to God's purpose would call for some changes in my thinking and actions. Now, please remember that I had to adjust my thinking of being a beaten, bruised, and battered person who had no hope left within me. I had to realize that God had not changed His will for my life. God's will had been and still is for me to preach, teach, and speak His glorious truths. Remember also that I had once been offered an ultimatum. If I would turn my back on God's call in my life, maybe I could keep my family intact. I had refused that offer, and the choice of keeping my covenant with God made a profound difference. I had only one thing left to do—I had to act on that decision. As James 2:17-18 says, *"Even so faith, if it has no works, is dead, being by itself. But someone may well say, you have faith and I have works; show me your faith without the works, and I will show you my faith by works"*.

Strangely enough, God had chosen to bring about a series of events that would prove His will for my life. These events would serve me in a provisional way yet teach me that victory comes with a price—a price I must be willing to pay and a price for which I will accept responsibility.

The first victory was that within the church membership was a lady who worked as an accountant. She came to me and asked, "How would you feel about training as a tax consultant for farmers and ranchers?"

My reply was, "Why not? But will I have time to pursue establishing a distribution company as well?"

The answer, of course, was "yes"; so Lois Carr and I became business partners. What I did not realize was that this lady was not just an accountant. She had the largest clientele in the area—over four hundred thirteen accounts. Lois also did tax preparation for the general public. So, during the first four to five months of the year I served as a consultant to farmers and ranchers, helping them find and document items, those which could be listed as qualified deductions.

I had previously inquired about and received an agreement to become a products distributor for Lemon Chill, which was owned by Moore Enterprises of Fort Worth, Texas. Lemon Chill had been introduced and sold in theme parks like Six Flags over Texas as well as at the Ballpark in Arlington and the Fort Worth Zoo. The product had not, however, been introduced into the retail market as had ice cream novelties. I posed a question to Moore Enterprises, "If Lemon Chill can outperform Coke in sales at theme parks, why should it not be in every home freezer like ice cream?"

That was a good question. Again the answer was "yes"; so from May to October I marketed and distributed Lemon Chill products. The result of this endeavor was that, against all odds, I outsold Six Flags over Texas and the Ballpark in Arlington in Lemon Chill for the next five years—1991-1996. The amazing part of this success story is that after I had become the largest distributor on the independent basis, I began to receive contracts to distribute ice cream for brand name companies who furnished products to all the accounts in major chain corporations. Suddenly I had an interest in an accounting firm, where I was learning valuable tax structure, and owned a distribution company worth more than $300,000 per year. What more could a person ask for?

Well, I asked for one more thing. I prayed, "God, could I please get a place to preach your Word?" He said "Yes!" A small rural church just out of Cisco needed a preacher, and—can you believe this—they would actually let a divorced preacher speak in God's house! What a victory! I had reached another level of acceptance.

My journey back into the world had begun to bring positive and provisional experiences. My children had not come around very much since they left—in fact, not at all. They did, however, still live in Cisco; and I would see them drive by my house and office occasionally. That was all right. At least I knew they were alive and looked OK.

I found out another thing about kids, especially teenagers. They like money! One day I saw both of them and said, "Come by the office. I have something to give you." Now curiosity must have gotten the best of them, as they had seen the office and a company form and delivery trucks multiply. Being fairly intelligent, they came by to see me. I had placed them on the payroll of the company so that when they did come by and do work, they could earn some money and at the same time become a part of what God had blessed me with. And this became a tax deduction! Wow! I was seeing the kids, sharing a business, and getting a tax write-off all at the same time! What a victory!

Eventually all this success became a point of interest to others, and after several years I received an offer to sell out. By now I had recovered financially and had started preaching fairly regularly on a fill-in or interim basis. I also had begun to pray about making a change in location. I decided to accept the buyout offer and began to make preparations to move either back home to DeKalb or to someplace where I could make a fresh start. The kids had reached a point in their lives where they did not mind coming by to get a paycheck, but spending time with me was not in their thoughts. I accepted that because they were now somewhat older and married and on their own.

Strangely, one day before leaving West Texas to make my fresh start, my telephone rang. I answered in my usual way, "Speak up, it's your nickel!" I tempered my response with a slight chuckle of course.

The reply came, "Larry, guess who."

I have this uncanny ability to remember faces, names, and voices. I responded, "I think this must be my long-lost cousin Carol."

"Yep." She said, "I have kind of kept up with you through the grapevine and understand you are thinking about coming toward East Texas. Is that correct?"

"Yes."

She then asked, "If you are coming this way, would you like to stop by and visit for a day or two so we can catch up on things? After all, it has been ten years."

I thought for a quick minute (about two seconds) and accepted the invitation. "You know, that sounds great. Where are you now?"

She informed me, "I'm in Denison, Texas, right on your way to DeKalb. Call me when you get in town and I'll give you directions to the house."

The next thing Carol, my sweet interested cousin, said to me before hanging up the phone would set into motion a whole new chain of events that God would use to return me to a purpose driven life for His glory. She said, "Larry, I also have a friend I'd like for you to meet. OK? Hello! Larry, are you there?"

"Yes, Carol," I stammered. "I'm here. But you know I might not be ready for this. I do, however, want to come see you. It's been a long time."

In a couple of days I made my way to Denison and called Carol. She came to meet me so I could follow her to her house, and the reunion began. We sat on the patio drinking the coffee she had made. Unknown to me, she had also made a phone call to one of her teacher friends.

As we sat on the patio reminiscing about the past ten years, the door bell rang and Carol got up to open the door. Standing there was the most absolutely beautiful embodiment of a woman I had ever seen.

During those dark and distorted years of my life, I was not able to recognize what a beautiful person would even resemble. It has been said that "the eyes are the windows to our souls." I find this to be truer today than ever before. The eyes make contact and they tell a story all its own. When I looked into the eyes of this beautiful creature of God, her eyes told a book full. What would you expect from a guy who has just begun to look at the world in a completely different way?

At the time I did not quite know how to act because it had been such a long time since I had been introduced to a member of the opposite sex with the prospect of dating her. In fact, it had been eleven years. All I had done was work, make money, and interact with businessmen and women. A person in the business world does not see anyone in regard to a relationship when he or she is attempting to build a resourceful and powerful business reputation. I had accomplished this in many ways without the glitter and glamour, just old-fashioned hard work and a "can-do" attitude! I had realized that in the early years of the ministry the biggest effect on my approach to winning people to Christ was the attitude that there was no one out of the reach of the plan of salvation, God's grace is all sufficient. I applied the same attitude and principles to the business world, and brother, did it work! I had been asked by a couple of large business corporations along with Lemon Chill to train their corporate sales staff and independent distributors. Well, I could write another book right here about how God had changed many things in my life especially the way to work and make money. But I want to get back to this beautiful and desirable person that was standing in front of me with our eyes locked on each other.

I was awestruck by what I saw in the doorway. I still am! My focus still was completely on fulfilling God's purpose in my life, and I just love what God gave me next. Psalms37: 3-4 state "Trust in the Lord, and do good; dwell in the land and cultivate faithfulness. Delight yourself in the Lord; and He will give you the desires of your heart."

Two words in these verses jumped off the pages at me are "dwell" and "cultivate." These are terms that every farmer or businessman is fully attentive to in order to become successful and influential at what he is doing. I had to come to know the difference between being alone and being lonely. The state of being lonely can be easily cured, just go out there and interact with people! The demands that this can create will astound one beyond measure, especially if what one is doing is proving to be profitable and successful. The state of being alone is completely different. I would go to the place where I lived, some call it home, and the only person there was me! That is being alone!

What stood in front of me was the person that was going to change both of those characteristics in my life. I was beginning to think about sticking around to see who this lovely creature was. This can be pictured by the word "dwell," the generation today I think call it "hanging out together." Also my desire to "cultivate" a relationship began to cross my mind. When I saw Barbara, I thought, "She tripped my trigger" and "She melted my butter."

The meeting between Barbara and me was one of all the right stuff, even though I was at a point of growth in my distribution company and a relationship would be a long-distance relationship, I believed that it would be time well invested toward the future. So, after spending the entire afternoon getting acquainted with her and talking with two wonderful ladies, we all decided to go out to eat and then call it a day. However, before saying good night I asked if she, Barbara, would like to have a date with me if I stayed over an extra night. The answer came as a pleasant yes.

God began that day to bless us with the wonderful, joyful, and peaceful relationship that we still have today. I truly believe that one essential element of love is patience. God had shown me the need to be careful regarding what I allowed to come into my life. I guess one could say I was cautious about any relationship possibility and yet I was excited about meeting Barbara. The Word of God had been a big influence in guiding my decision-making process.

First Corinthians 13: 4-7 says, "Love is patient, love is kind, and is not jealous; love does not brag and is not arrogant, does not act unbecomingly; it does not seek its own, is not provoked, does not take into account wrong, does not rejoice in unrighteousness, but rejoices with the truth; bears all things, believes all things, hopes all things, endures all things."

The importance of putting into practice these verses of Scripture would prove to be one of the most stabilizing forces in our relationship. My life had suffered many years of emptiness, darkness, and loneliness, but now God had brought me someone full of His love and radiant in person. I was immediately attracted; still I developed the patience to allow love to grow and prove itself as the above Scripture says. In fact, I dated Barbara four years before asking her to become my wife.

The years that I spent in the emotional turmoil of anger, depression, and feeling abandoned by family and friends were so difficult. Some of those friends were those so-called church folk who hang their Christian credentials on being a church member faithful and true right down to the last dollar. During the emotional turmoil I found myself in a huge downward spiral that made me vulnerable to many temptations and this is exactly the time and place in my life that Satan attacked me the hardest. If you ever find yourself in this position, do three very important things which are these:

(1) Pray without ceasing that God put a hedge of protection around you.

(2) Search the Holy Bible for Scriptures of strength and power.

(3) Abide in the fellowship of true believers so you can find the support and encouragement you need.

Barbara and her mother were sitting in the swing of Barbara's patio talking about their trip from Kansas, where Barb's mother lives. Barbara had brought her mother to Texas for a visit. Hazel was in her eighties at that time and still very healthy and sharp-witted. I came up to the swing where they sat talking, walked around to the back of the swing until I was behind Barb, then reached around and held the engagement ring I had purchased in front of her, and Hazel looked me straight in the eye and said:

"Well, it's about time! Larry, you are slower than the seven year itch!"

To which I replied, "No, Hazel, I have dated Barb for only four years, not seven!"

But it was an itch that I wanted Barb to scratch. Of course Hazel said yes, and this relationship is the most fulfilling partnership that I could have prayed for in my return to life's purposing and performing of God's will. On July 21, 2002, Barbara became Mrs. Larry Linam; and it was for me another wonderfully sweet victory! Sorry, Honey, I meant to say, "It IS a wonderfully sweet victory!"

The covenant relationship that Barb and I have is so open and honest with each other that life has become one great partnership with full collaboration for each of us. One day, after several years of marriage, I came in from my business and asked Barb if she would consider retiring from teaching and move to DeKalb, Texas. My parents live there and are getting on up in their years. I wanted to go home and help care for them and take my boot and shoe-repair business into that community. Barb had taught in public education for thirty-six years and had reached the magic numbers needed to draw full retirement benefits from the Texas Retirement System. So, after praying about the matter, we decided to make the move because we strongly felt God's leading in that direction. So we made a phone call to my mom and dad and informed them of our decision, which made them extremely happy. Can you imagine that! Parents just tickled pink to see their kids coming back into their lives after having raised and tolerated all they had done to them in life! Well, God put His hand on the circumstances and just did what only God can do.

Barb and I wanted to continue to preach, teach, and do music in a church setting. God was working in our lives and in a church just seven miles north of DeKalb. The Spring Hill Baptist Church had been searching for a pastor for several months. I contacted a member of the church and asked if it would be permissible for me to mail my resumé to the pastoral search committee, which I did the next day. One week later the chairman of the search committee contacted me by telephone and extended an invitation to meet with the committee. I served as pastor and Barbara as the adult Sunday school teacher and church pianist. I knew this church very well, for I had delivered the second sermon I ever preached in this very church in the summer of 1967, after I graduated from the DeKalb High School.

We have been serving this church for the past four years on a bi-vocational basis. Barbara and I began a business called Texoma Boot & Shoe Repair and Sales in February 2006. I had learned the trade skill of boot-and shoe-repair while going to college and had maintained the trade during the past seventeen years. God put His hand of blessing on this as well, and the business was a success from its first day in operation. I have always been one to focus on making anything I endeavor to do a ministry of witness or testimony to His glory.

Three weeks after opening the business, tragedy struck. March 26, 2006 around 8:00 p.m. the telephone at my parents' house rings. I was there eating the evening meal with them after church. The voice on the other end of the line said, "Irene, tell Larry that the building next to his shop is on fire!"

I could hear the voice on the phone, so I dropped my fork and immediately got into my truck and headed for my business. As I approached the business district, I could see all the fire engines, police, and emergency vehicles around the building that was engulfed in flames. The firefighters were frantically moving to get into positions where the flames were pouring out of the building faster than the water was pouring in.

I walked near a large group of firefighters and heard some comments that were not good news to me. The chief said, "Men, the wind is picking up and it's out of the north. We need to concentrate on the south side of the building."

The south side of the building that was on fire was connected to the building that housed my boot-and shoe-repair operations. The wind picked up with increasing speed and began to fan the flames directly into my business. Thirty-eight minutes later both the building where the fire started and my business lay on the ground in a charred pile of burnt wood and brick. To me, it was so devastating and what hit my mind next was a blessing. I instantly thought that the devil attacks in areas that can really hurt us and this apparently was a real effort to move against what God had brought about for us to be in the ministry.

Once again God gave me a sense of dry wit and humor. A friend of mine came up to my side as I stood in the street looking at the flames and embers that had just leveled my business and means of income. He said, "Gee, Larry, I am so sorry for all this to happen to you and you were just getting started in your business. Is there anything I can do?"

I said to my friend, "Do you have any money on you and is the grocery store still open?"

"Yes, I do, and yes the store is still open."

"OK, hurry down to the store before it closes and buy us some buns, mustard, and franks!"

"Why," my friend asked with a puzzled look on his face.

"This is just too good of a fire to waste!" I said.

Forty-five days later, I had found a place to relocate and had completed the remodeling of the old building that stood on some property that was located on the main highway going through the small town of DeKalb. I had driven past this location dozens of times and had never thought that anything could be done with it or that it might be for sale. I knew the owner of the property. It occurred to me that it might be just the spot for a new shop location. I got in my truck and drove to the owner's place of business, went in and inquired about purchasing the property.

Our Lord is so gracious and right on time! Thirty minutes later, I wrote the owner of that property a check for the land and building. It just happened to be one of the prime locations of property in the city on Highway 82, a main travel route east and west across the southern part of the United States. I had great insurance and it paid off. I now have a newly remodeled place of business in a prime location and new equipment and it is debt free! Boy, what a great fire!

The three years after the rebuilding from this challenge proved to be exciting as God put His hand of blessing on the business and the church. Barbara and I had planned, worked, and managed with diligence. The spirit of the church is progressing, and the business is profitable beyond our expectations!

One day, as I was at home taking a day off, the phone rang. I picked up the cordless phone and answered in the usual fashion.

"Good morning, this is Larry Linam."

The voice on the other end said, "Larry, this is Billy Foote, I have had you on my mind, and thought I would give you a call since finding you listed on the internet."

Billy Foote was one of my long-time acquaintances and an evangelist. I had not seen him for several years. As a matter of fact, I had briefly spoken with him in Sherman, Texas, and that meeting was for just a few minutes. It had been twenty years since we had any time to really talk about the events of our lives.

"This is a real surprise," I responded. "Why have I been on your mind?"

Billy said, "Larry, I have been speaking across the country in several meetings about how families are facing very tragic circumstances such as you have faced in your life and I have been telling people about how God has brought you through some of the worst elements that a person could face."

"Well, what has been the response of the people?" I asked.

The answer Billy Foote gave me set in motion the next challenge that God had in store for me. He said, "Larry, people want to know what has happened to you and I would like to meet with you to discuss the possibilities of you telling your story."

I then told Billy, "I wrote a book some years ago and strangely enough it is about the very things you are asking me. I called it 'The Day Angels Cried' and if you would like to meet that will be fine with me."

So the meeting was set for us to meet in Mount Pleasant, Texas, at a local restaurant on the following Monday morning. God set into motion on that day a plan and a challenge to bring this work in book form and personal testimony to a new level and to a place and time that He has intended for His glory all along. After this initial meeting God has begun to open doors for Billy Foote and me to deliver a wonderful message of deliverance and forgiveness—The deliverance from the awful and terrible emotion of anger that possessed me, robbed me, and isolated me for many years. The forgiveness that God had toward me personally and the forgiveness that I was able to extend was a result of being forgiven.

Billy and Winky Foote have been a wonderful and blessed encouragement to me. They have prayed for this work, attended the meetings as they would help schedule them, and gave very important advice to me in refining the delivery of the message and invitation for individuals, parents, and families to draw closer to God's purpose and plan for them. I will never be able to thank them enough. I know this for certain, when God lays a challenge before us, He truly prepares the way with the proper people, the proper means, and the proper time!

However, there were other challenges facing me as a result of God opening this new frontier. Barbara and I had seen a small boot-and shoe-repair operation grow into a strong retail operations offering Western boots, work boots, and hunting boots for sale. The business had gotten larger in its demands than the two of us could handle, along with my being in the pastorate. And now we were faced with traveling to speak in other churches on a limited schedule. We needed some help!

Barbara and I began praying. We had asked God to send us the right people to help us with the business. One week later Melanie Payne sat in our living room sharing a burden in her life for which she needed a resolution. She is a certified registered pharmacy technician and wanted to make a change. As we shared our thoughts and experiences with her, I looked at her and said:

"Melanie, maybe it is time you did something to suit yourself and that would benefit you more than working for someone else."

I did not know what affect that might have on her but a few days later it became apparent.

Melanie and Dickie Payne have always been very involved in the Spring Hill Baptist Church, and in the Four States Fair and Rodeo. Melanie is a former Miss Four States Fair and Rodeo Queen. Folks, this is a big deal around this neck of the woods! They came walking into the business not long after our discussion in the living room of our home. Both of them had expressed an interest in the business since I had trained their son, Chase, in the skill of boot-and shoe-repair. Chase is a natural at this skill. He took to this craft like a duck takes to water. It was at this time that God answered our prayer for help.

Dickie said, "Larry, we are interested in coming into the business as partners if you and Barbara are open to the idea."

I looked at Barbara as she looked back at me as if to say, "God sure does work in ways that are unmistakably clear."

We spent the next two or three evenings discussing all the possibilities and details of creating a partnership. In order to do this properly and with transparency, we all wanted to be sure that the business plan would fit everyone's expectations. The match was good, the people were good, and the business is healthy to stand the load. God put together a great combination of people in Barbara and Larry Linam along with Melanie and Dickie Payne to make a bigger and better Texoma Boot & Shoe Repair and Sales team. Now on to the issue of the church and my bi-vocational status.

The fact that God has begun a work of reaching out to people suffering from the stress of traumatic events across our great country has brought me to a point of telling this story of deliverance and forgiveness. I have come to realize that holding the position of a bi-vocational pastor is complicated by being absent from the church pulpit more than one should be. The membership of the church, however, is very supportive and excited about what God is doing with their pastor. The needs of a church, even the size of Spring Hill Baptist Church, still remains and should be met and I realized I could not fulfill the needs and go out to other churches and speak the message that God had placed in my heart and mind. It has been said that "parting is such sweet sorrow." I began to feel this as I realized that God was moving me into a new venture of ministry. I have completed four years of wonderful living among some of the greatest people in church. But I made the difficult decision to step out on faith to speak this new message of hope for those suffering from the attack of Satan and the trauma that evil deeds bring to people's lives. This decision to retire from the pastorate has come after thirty-four years of service, but a new horizon and a new vision are before me.

In conclusion, my prayer has shifted from asking God to give me an awareness of the needs of a particular church to that of keeping me focused on the emotions that seem to be besetting people and families across the land. The Bible tells us that God is not the author of confusion and the horrible turmoil that comes to us in the midst of posttraumatic stress is one of the contributors to our lives becoming a nightmare of unimaginable proportion. I have lived for years with feelings of hopelessness, depression, and isolation and anger. But God, who is so rich and merciful, still brings people like me back from the clutches of Satan and makes us useful and productive. I look forward to life's challenges in helping others deal with the hurt and sorrow that our world brings. Maybe someday, somewhere our paths will cross. I can find no better way to end this work of telling my life's story except to say that there is no person whom the Lord of lords and King of kings cannot reach, redeem, and completely restore to a peaceful, joyful, and fulfilling life that will bring blessings to one's life and great glory to our Lord and Savior, Jesus Christ.

Chapter 10 – Finding Forgiveness

The journey of writing this book is one that just never seems to end or ceases to amaze me. It has been one of unending discovery of the hours and even days of remembering, thinking, reliving in my mind, writing, and encountering new experiences of dealing with people from the past. The most significant thing I have faced in this whole ordeal of bearing my soul to you has been finding God's purpose and plan for my life as I enter what some folks call the latter stages of living. I am convinced that a person who seeks to serve God's purpose for his or her life will always face challenges in which many demands for action and adaptation will present themselves at almost every turn.

In 2007, a friend of mine, Steve McMichael, invited me to a seminar his church was hosting. Steve and his wife, Michelle, are the founders and pastors of the Maranatha Ministries located in DeKalb, Texas. During this seminar I came to face the importance of forgiveness. In the small group sessions each group would meet and read and answer questions in the textbook. What was said and conveyed in the small group sessions were to remain in that confidential status of the group. I had been in vocational ministry for several decades and knew that this agreement might work and then it might not; it just depended on the men in the room. However, the group of men were intent on keeping the agreement. One of the lessons in the seminar was on forgiveness. I knew that this one would be a tough one for me because I had been hiding within me as best I could a lot of unforgiveness.

I had not forgiven many people for some very difficult things that had been done to me and said to me. The problem is that anger is the best friend of an unforgiving spirit. I had discovered that I could stuff this down inside myself for certain periods of time. However, at different times this monster would rise up and exhibit itself. Many times it would leave no doubt in anyone's mind that a nerve had been struck, and usually the results were not comfortable to say the least. As each member of the men's group began to tell of some of the things that each wanted to bring to a point of forgiveness, I began to think of what was really making me angry. There I discovered that I had never forgiven certain people for the death of my daughter.

The conversation was filled with spiritual tones and confessions as each member of the small group shared testimonies of circumstances that each had kept to himself. As each one conveyed his thoughts, I knew my time was approaching. I began to think about this as the opportunity drew closer and closer to me as it moved around the table. How could I tell of the anger I had kept for years toward a man who was no longer alive? What would I say that would give these men the impression that a local pastor had at least a form of having a forgiving spirit about him? What would they think of me if I just said what my true feelings really were about myself? As my time to face reality came, I could refuse to make any comment or come face to face with the opportunity to let God do a work in my heart and mind! Steve was sitting to my left and he had shared some things with the group that had been troubling him about forgiveness. I thought, if he can have the courage and heart desire to bring his to the table, I need to come out with mine as well.

My time came and I sat for just a brief moment. I looked up and all eyes were fastened on me, or so it seemed as I looked around the table. A quick prayer, I spoke in my mind, "Lord, help me to get this right and give me an open heart and mind."

"Gentlemen," I said, "I have something that I have been carrying around with me for more than twenty years. I have tried and succeeded at stuffing this problem of forgiveness down and have allowed this anger to eat away at my personality, my spirit as a Christian, and my thoughts in daily life too long. I want to get it out in the open and I will need your prayers and understanding for I have never spoken about this to anyone in all my past years."

You could have heard a pin drop. All eyes and ears seemed to be fastened on me. I looked to my best friend in the room and I see a look of confidence as well as true concern on his face. He then just nodded as if to say, "go ahead and put it on the table, God will take it and use it for our good and yours as well."

I began by saying, "I do not know how to forgive a dead man except to say that I am doing just this right now! I do not want to carry this heavy load of anger anymore! I want forgiveness for all my angry thoughts and actions carried out against Al King's family, the man who murdered my daughter in 1980. The presence of this unforgiving spirit in me has been like a ghost haunting me for more than two decades, and I want to be done with it forever! Please pray for me and with me!"

Would you believe it! Steve spoke up and said to the group, "let's pray for Larry now." The men around the table bowed their heads and began to pray with me and for me as Steve led us in prayer.

I do not know everything about God's moving or plans for us in this world, but I do know that this time and event was like no other.

I felt as if another curtain of darkness had just been raised up and light filled the emptiness within me. I remember that no thoughts of how to get back, no thoughts of vengeance remained, and I felt I could even breathe better. Had I known what God was going to do with this in that moment, I would have done this many years ago!

The small group session then went from the classroom to the fellowship area. I was standing in the hallway talking with several of the men in the crowd of people when Steve came up and asked if he could have a word with me. My thoughts went back to a time when a counselor said that what took place in the First Baptist Church of Daingerfield was too hard for people to grasp or imagine, and that I should keep it to myself. However, this was not the case this time. Steve approached me with a look of kindness and love.

Steve said, "Larry, this is a story that I feel the Lord can use this to touch the lives of people, and you should consider sharing it with the entire church during out next meeting with everyone. Would you be willing to tell the full story of your testimony?"

My thoughts immediately went to the idea that people would think I was demented with nothing but pure hate and anger in my heart. I then remembered what we had just prayed for and what I had felt. I thought to myself, this is exactly what the devil tries to do in order to keep me from doing my best for God's will in my life. I looked at Steve with eyes of hope and question.

"How about sharing your story in our next general assembly tomorrow night?" Steve asked.

I replied, "that is fine with me. I will begin to put my thoughts together and be ready when you call me to the stage."

The next night I took the stage after Steve announced that the small group sessions would not be meeting so that I would have time to tell the full story of my life. The crowd was large and seemed to have an air of expectancy about them as all eyes were fastened on me. I began to tell the story of the shootings and murders that occurred on June 22, 1980, in the First Baptist Church, Daingerfield, Texas, and then proceeded to take them through a step-by-step process of my life covering more than two decades. I spoke for one and a half hours and yet not one person moved during the entire time. I began to notice that some had moved to the front of their seats, while I could hear others weeping and see them wiping tears from their eyes. I ended the story by telling that I asked the men's small group to pray for me as I sought to give forgiveness and to seek forgiveness from those whom I had offended in past years. The impact of that statement must have been like a lightning bolt. It struck a note of concern for many people because on ending the delivery of my testimony, I asked Steve to come and take charge of the service and offer a time of public decision for anyone wanting to come forward. The musicians began to play softly while parents, young people, and others began to come forward to pray and make decisions of commitment for God's will in their lives. At this point I realized that God had placed in me a story of forgiveness and that I had to give myself to sharing it wherever an invitation came.

The one thing that remained was that element of *finding forgiveness*. It is easy to say in a prayer that I wanted forgiveness for all the horrible things I had said and done in the past toward those involved with the man who had taken the life of my daughter. However, sometimes it is not enough to pray for forgiveness; one needs to seek and ask forgiveness as well.

The invitation for decisions was not just for others because it became clear that I had a decision to make about forgiveness. At this time, I stepped to the front with Steve at my side and I said, "I am going to need your prayers and support because I now have to find the family of the man who murdered my daughter and ask for forgiveness for my attempts to harm them in the years following the event that occurred in the First Baptist Church, Daingerfield, Texas. I need to say that I am sorry for bringing legal action against an innocent lady and for the physical assault attempted on an innocent young man. I must find them, look them in the eye, and beg forgiveness from them."

On making that statement, many in the crowd lifted their hands into the air, began applauding, and agreeing with what I said. It was like a holy verification from above that God was in this place and speaking to me. I had come full circle. What had began more than twenty years ago in hatred and vengeance was now replaced with hope and God's love. The disparity and darkness just left me and God replaced it with joy, life, and peace. I had been waiting a long time for this to happen, and now it was done. I was ready to move on!

MOVE ON! Two little words, yet these are words that came to be very significant for me. They were significant in three ways. First, I had placed this book, "The Day the Angels Cried" on a shelf for the past eighteen months. It was incomplete, not in its content but because I was not what God could use to tell the story. A story of this nature and impact must come from a pure heart and mind that is willing to be guided and governed by God's purpose.

Second, I had to get all of life's distractions out of the way. I needed to become focused on the purpose of telling a story not just centered around a single event but on life of coming from darkness and destruction to love, joy, and peace; while remembering that Satan will most assuredly attack the whole process as hard as he can to stop it.

Third, I could now begin the search for the family members of the man who murdered my daughter. This would not be a search to bring harm to them but a sincere effort to find them, to speak with them, and *find forgiveness* from them.

I immediately began the search. The most obvious place to begin was where the event took place. I journeyed back to Daingerfield. This was a hard trip because no matter how hard one tries to block out bad things, it does not always happen. I stepped out of my truck as I pulled up in front of the First Baptist Church in Daingerfield only to see the beautiful monument placed in front of the church with the names of all those who had lost their lives that day. I quickly moved past the monument and into the church office to meet with the pastor. He invited me into his office and after a few minutes I asked him if he had any knowledge of the family members of the man who had committed the murders in the church on June 22, 1980.

The response was direct and immediate, "Larry, it is strange that you would ask that because just a month ago the daughter of the man who murdered your daughter called me and asked to come speak to the church because she felt she needed to let people here know that she was concerned for them and how much she had hated what had happened so long ago."

I asked, "Do you know where she is and how I might contact her?"

"No", he replied, "and she would not tell me where she was calling from. Maybe, because I had told her that some folks still had some hard feelings about the circumstances."

After exchanging other points of interest and having shared with the pastor that I had written this book, he asked me if I would be interested in addressing the church when the book was published. I told him I would love to begin the issuing of the book in the very place where it all began. I considered this a victory in itself. But I still did not know how to find what I really came for—the family of the man who murdered my daughter.

I began to make inquiries around Daingerfield over the next several months as I went back at times, only to come up with dead ends on leads. A stroke of luck came my way on the third trip. I found one of my best friends when I lived in Daingerfield and I asked about some of the families, because he knew almost everyone in town. As we talked, he told me that Mrs. Gretchen King had moved to Avinger and joined the Methodist church there. I could not wait to get into the truck and head in that direction, for it was only a few miles to Avinger, arriving in Avinger, I asked a few people about Mrs. King but I came up empty handed for my efforts.

I came back home late that evening a little discouraged and asking God to help me find these people. I know that God knows all things about all people and all the time. So I figured that God would be the best source of information.

Several months had passed as I had become busy with rewriting the book and speaking in churches in East Texas. My friend, Billy Foote, kept on encouraging me to be patient about finding the people I was looking for because God would bring all things together for good and at the proper time. I was okay with that statement and believed as he said, I had to wait for God's purposes to take place.

During this time Barbara and I had decided we would begin looking for a house since we felt that I needed to focus more on the book and telling the story. One day we decided to travel to Texarkana, a large city not far from us, to look at modular homes and some double-wide mobile homes. The first place we stopped had been recommended to us because of the type of homes they had were of high quality and they were reputable in their dealings with people. As Barbara and I went into the office, we were promptly met be a man who was very outgoing in his personality. The amazing element about coming into this place was that unknown to us, divine appointment was at work. The first thing I noticed on the walls of this salesman's office were the framed photos of him with some high-ranking dignitaries such as a former president of the United States and other well-known congressmen. Also on the walls were photos of this salesman in the prestigious Carnegie Hall where he had performed classical music. This guy was not an ordinary salesman. He was a man with a story! We sat and talked about what we had come there to do and what type of home we would be interested in. After a few minutes of shop talk, I changed the course of the conversation. Or should I say, the spirit of God directed the conversation into another direction.

I asked, "Is that a picture of Carnegie Hall? Is this a picture of you and a former president of the United States of America?"

To which he replied, "Yes to both of your questions".

He then added that some unique circumstances were behind all the photos on his walls. He conveyed to me that God had lifted him out of some of the worst circumstances a person could face in life. He continued to share how he had come from high-ranking political status to becoming involved in some legal matters that led him into prison. I then noticed that at one time he had been an attorney and I began to feel as though God had brought us together for a very special reason.

The salesman then asked, "Why all the interest in what is hanging on my walls?"

I then began to tell this man that I too had come through some very hard circumstances in life and have written a book. The conversation continued toward sharing what difficulties we had experienced in life and that we had many things in common. However, when I shared with him that one of the things I had to come to was *finding forgiveness* from some folks he asked the obvious question.

"What do you have to ask forgiveness for?"

I told him that I was searching for a lady by the name of Mrs. Gretchen King, the widow of the man who had murdered my daughter during the shootings at the First Baptist Church in Daingerfield, Texas. He looked at me with a look of faintness as his mouth seemed to drop to the floor. I asked him if there was something wrong and he replied,

"I know this lady and as a matter of fact, I am her Sunday school teacher. I have known her for a long time because she was also one of my children's teachers in school."

The shock on both our faces was easy to recognize as we looked at each other. I had been searching for this lady to do what God had put in my heart about seeking forgiveness but I could not find her but now I was sitting in front of a man who could lead me to her. I knew then and now that God has more excellent and higher ways than I did. God had put a plan and a purpose into motion. He was in full control of the circumstances!

In a state of sheer amazement I said, "Could you tell me where she lives or how I can get in touch with her?"

Picking up his cell phone, he replied, "I can get her phone number for you right now, and I don't mind telling you that the hair on the back of my neck is standing up!"

I got the phone number of the one person I needed to speak with, and then Barbara and I toured some homes we wanted to see. The one thing that became clear was that this was no ordinary meeting. The stop we made this day was God's way of saying that He is in control.

A few days passed before I decided to make that call to Gretchen King. My heart was pounding inside my chest with the mounting excitement of being able to speak the words that I had so needed to say for a long time. The phone rang and an answering machine picked up, and I left a message telling who I was, why I was calling, and my cell phone number. After hanging up, I thought to myself, if someone called me that had in past years had tried to bring harm to my family over an event that she had been victimized herself would you call this man. I think not! So, to add some reassurance to the situation I sat down and wrote a letter after obtaining her mailing address.

The days passed, three of them to be exact, and no phone call. I was standing near the location where Barbara and I are having a new home built when the phone rang. The voice on the other end was a woman's voice that said,

"Larry, this is Gretchen King, and I got your letter this morning and read it, and I felt that I needed to make this call to you."

The joy and excitement that came over me was indescribable. I began to share my heart's desire with her and told her I had waited for this time to come with a lot of hope. The words of my heart and mind just flowed like a river. It was one of the most fulfilling conversations I have ever had with anyone. This was a phone call with divine impact!

The amazing thing about this call was what happened the next day. The next evening while sitting in my favorite chair the phone rang. As I picked up the receiver the voice said,

"Larry, this is the daughter of Gretchen King and I want to speak with you for a while. OK?"

Now I was speaking to the second person God had put on my list to talk to! Needless to say, the conversation was just as welcomed and wonderful as any phone call could possibly be. As the conversation ended, we agreed to stay in touch. When I hung up the phone, I told Barbara that I felt as if I had come full circle in my life. It feels like a true sense of completion.

On Saturday, September 5, 2009, I put my arms around Gretchen King. The release of fear, the hatred of the past, and the painful memories had already been gone, but the whole world seemed to get better and brighter at this particular time. I had put into action the thoughts of *finding forgiveness.* I was not seeking a person to bring harm to reality but I was embracing a person in joy and kindness. I was looking into the face of a person that God loved and gave his only Son upon the cross for, just like He did for me! Instead of being torn further apart by hate and horror, two people were being bonded together by this exciting divine appointment!

I know that many people will not view all these events as nothing more than everyday things that can happen when someone wants to make things right. But this could not be applied to me in this matter. I still have one person with whom to reconnect and I am confident that in the coming days this too, will happen. I also know that never has the story that I will tell to hopefully thousands of people who are hurting with severe tragedies and traumatic loss be more needed than it is today. I pray that God will open doors for me, to share with others not only this story but a personal word of encouragement that God is still on the throne and has the power to lift us out of darkness, depression, and despair. What once was a life of torment ruled by so many negative elements, is now a life with hope and desire to bring the wonderful sense and feeling of peace coupled with the excitement of an eternal reunion of our loved ones. **GOD BLESS!**

CONTACT INFORMATION

If you or your civic organization would like to contact Larry Linam to have him come and speak to your church or group please call or e-mail at:

    Phone: 903-667-0998   e-mail: lclinam@yahoo.com

THE REUNION

By Larry Linam

I Thessalonians 4: 16-18 (NASB) "For the Lord Himself will descend
from heaven with a shout, with the voice of the archangel, and with
the trumpet of God; and the dead in Christ shall rise first. Then we
who are alive and remain shall be caught up together with them in
the clouds to meet the Lord in the air, and thus we shall always be
with the Lord. Therefore comfort one another with these words."

My life has been filled with many events
With the passing of the days.
Some have been good, some have been bad
But God has led me through in many ways.

But I still sit and watch the morning come,
Drinking coffee and missing you.
Recalling your beautiful smile on your sweet face,
Remembering the voice and sounds such as the case.

So I sit and watch the clouds roll in
From the distance and from the east.
They look unusual, moving fast and illuminated
Not dark to say the least.

Then all of a sudden, a shout so loud
That it shook the ground!
And then came the blast
Of a trumpet sound.

129

The clouds rolled back and I saw a clear blue sky
And what I saw was beautiful to my eye.
A person stepped out into view upon the clouds
As the heavenly chorus sang aloud.

In an instant, the twinkling of an eye
I was moved from earth but did not die.
The joy, the brightness, and love I did feel
And all I had read of God's Word was now real.

The bonds of gravity were released and I moved
Through the clouds up in the sky.
And then I saw Jesus coming toward me with many angels
And precious souls who upon Him rely.

As Jesus came closer I could see His look of love
As I bowed down upon my knee.
Then he reached down, lifted me up and said,
"I have something for you to see."

I thought to myself,
"Oh, all Heaven I'm about to view!"
I could only imagine what beauty and wonders.
I would not know what to do.

We walked, we talked, as across Heaven we strolled
And I saw things the Bible has foretold.
I could see family and friends all along the way
We would hug and speak as we moved through the day.

But after what seemed an eternity
And I was still looking round
Jesus stood beside me and told me
"I have something for you that I have found."

Jesus said, "Larry, turn around."
And tell me what you see.
I said, "I see Heaven, peace, and love
With Jesus and me."

And as I continued to speak of what I saw
I felt something wonderful, a sense of awe.
I turned to look at Jesus and He stepped to my side
And the thrill and excitement, I could not hide!

There stood Gina alive and well,
No hurt, no pain only Heaven could tell.
She looked at me with that beautiful smile and said,
"Hi Daddy,, I've been waiting to see you for awhile."

It seemed that all Heaven broke out in a song
As we hugged and kissed for so long.
We walked, we talked in my arms she did rest.
THE REUNION in Heaven will no doubt be blest.

Epilogue – Dr. Charles Vance

You have just read the true and personal story of Larry Linam, told in his own words, a man who survived the horror of the mass murder of five people and the wounding of ten others at First Baptist Church of Daingerfield, Texas during the morning worship service on June 22, 1980. One of the five people killed by a madman that traumatic day was Larry's seven-year-old daughter, Gina.

I came into this story in 1999, nineteen years after the traumatic event, when Larry sat down with me for the first time to tell his entire story. He opened a file and placed on the table a stack of magazines and newspaper clippings about the shooting at First Baptist of Daingerfield, Texas. He wanted to make sure I really knew what I was getting into by working with him. Looking back, I believe Larry was trying to see if I would become scared at the enormity of the trauma he had to deal with, and turn him away as others had. He began a journey that day with questions of possible hope for resolution and relief from the pain he carried for so long. In the weeks that followed, I heard a story that can best be described as a journey of horror that occurred that Sunday morning in June in Daingerfield. I look back and realize that the man before me, with all he was showing me, was a hurting man quietly screaming to me and God, "Is there any hope for me?"

To more fully understand the events of that tragic day, I asked Larry if he would take me to the scene of the tragedy. As I walked through the doors of First Baptist Church of Daingerfield with Larry as my guide, I felt a sense of disbelief as I came to stand in the very place where Al King yelled the words, "THIS IS WAR!" I stood with a strange sense of shock as Larry showed me where each person who died had been sitting or standing at the time King pulled the trigger on his weapon.

I stood just a few feet away from where little Gina Linam received her fatal wound. A few more feet away I saw the place where two of the murdered victims received their fatal wounds. I visualized around me the ten other people who were wounded and those who were lying on the floor crawling under the pews in fear.

Larry showed me where the substitute preacher of the day stood behind the pulpit and calmly told the people to get down, and then prayed, while the two large men of the church rushed the madman King to subdue him to save others' lives. I learned that there is no way to tell just how many other lives were saved as two men in the congregation became victims as they gave their own lives up to fatal gunshots. They pushed King out of the sanctuary, and away from the people gathered for peaceful worship that day. I saw and placed my fingers in the bullet holes, which on that day could still be found in the church building's walls.

As a pastor, I can hardly imagine what the new pastor must have felt on that day. There he was, home ill with a severe virus, instead of being in First Baptist Church taking the pulpit for his first Sunday as their new pastor. Only by the fact of his illness was he not there in the place of his substitute that day. His first act of pastoral ministry was to get out of his sickbed and arrive on the scene to begin to minister the wounded and the grief-stricken survivors.

Larry's visit to me was an additional attempt nineteen years later to sit down with someone for the specific purpose of dealing with the trauma in his life. Shortly after the mass murder of their daughter, Larry attended a group therapy session in Tyler, Texas, only to find their fellow group members stressed out over such earth-shattering struggles as "when to walk the dog," "what time to get up out of bed," and "where to go eat." It was this context of sharing the horror of the massacre at the First Baptist church of Daingerfield, that Larry had the disappointment of hearing a therapist tell him that she could not help anyone who had gone through such a horrible trauma. For eighteen years, Larry carried the belief that "No one can help me." He carried his trauma as a burden with no hope of ever finding relief.

When Larry met Barbara, a former client of mine, she asked Larry to come see me as their friendship became established. After the initial assessments were completed, I shared with Larry my therapeutic assessment and recommendations. On that day I witnessed a man discover hope for the first time in nineteen years, as I shared the reality of what I saw in his experience. I saw hope build as I explained what posttraumatic stress disorder is, and how to deal with it. I saw hope explode with tears of relief as I shared with Larry the reality of pain carried by victims of trauma as they experience what I called "frozen grief," and therefore live with incomplete healing from their trauma.

The syndrome of "frozen grief" is most commonly associated with traumatic events that are the cause of a loss, especially loss in the death of a loved one or loss of life goals. This condition can also occur when grief is blocked by preexisting mental and emotional conditions. The reality is that, rather than accomplishing the tasks of grief, grief can be abnormal, pathological, and complicated. Grief can be intensified, delayed, prolonged, and/or denied.

I believe that a grieving individual encounters four often difficult and time-consuming tasks:

- The need to accept the reality of the loss
- The ability to feel and consciously admit the pain of the loss. This includes untangling oneself from the ties that bind us to the deceased.
- Adjusting to an environment in which the deceased is missing.
- Forming new relationships.

The traumatic and senseless murder of his young daughter in the Sunday morning worship service of their church stopped Larry from accomplishing these grief tasks. The "frozen grief" kept Larry in bondage to his dead daughter and the unbelievable, traumatic means to her death. The "frozen grief" bondage prevented Larry from coping and moving on with his life.

Let me take a few pages to review just what kind of trauma could cause the kind of pain Larry had carried for years. On June 22, 1980, a peaceful, warm summer day in rural East Texas, at about 11:05 a.m., Alvin King entered the sanctuary of First Baptist Church in Daingerfield, Texas. He was armed for battle, standing at the rear of the sanctuary with both rifles and handguns. After shouting "THIS IS WAR!" he began to randomly shoot into the congregation. Within moments, five people were dead, including seven-year-old Gina Linam. King was quickly subdued by several men of the congregation and then arrested by the police as they rushed to the assistance of the men holding the murderer down.

The event, which lasted only a few moments, then evolved into weeks of unresolved, unrelenting, and ongoing traumatic events. King was put in the Rusk State Mental Hospital for court-ordered evaluation of psychiatric illness. The famous trial attorney, Percy Foreman, who was pushing an insanity defense, defended him. Every ninety-first day, there was a competency hearing to determine King's metal fitness. On the third competency hearing, King was judged competent to stand trial.

Alvin King, the man about to go to trial for the murder of Gina Linam and four others, was a schoolteacher and bus driver in the school system of Daingerfield. King had three PhD's from East Texas State University in Commerce, in the fields of math, science, and psychology. A look at the life of Al King shows a mix of psychological instability and probable criminal history.

- He was reported to be beating his wife.
- His daughter's fiancé was stabbed to death with seventeen wounds from an unknown assailant, after accusations of incest between King and his daughter had surfaced.
- At the time of the killings, the grand jury had delivered an indictment on seventeen counts of incest against King.
- There were arson accusations, based on the fact that King's last three houses were burned down.
- It was reported that at the age of twelve, King had decapitated his father by shooting him point-blank with a double-barrel 12-gauge shotgun.

With this kind of background and situation, Larry began to be fearful that the murderer of his daughter would not receive justice, because of a skillful lawyer's use of the insanity defense. During the nine months of competency evaluations Larry became obsessed with how to make sure Alvin King received justice, even if it meant Larry would have to kill King by himself. Larry had two fully planned and possible attempts to bring justice to King, stopped only by what is best described as providential action.

The fear of his daughter's murderer not coming to justice and the inability of Larry to resolve his trauma was strengthened and hardened when King died. Alvin King committed suicide after the third day of pre-trial hearings. He hung himself in his jail cell with strips torn form a bath towel.

Larry's entire pattern of behaviors now began to revolve around this traumatic event. The issues of posttraumatic stress disorder with Larry, like most trauma victims, left him with what I call "frozen grief." This "frozen life" lasted for nineteen years as Larry kept on carrying the pain of June 22, 1980. He coped with the trauma in the way that best suited his personality; he became withdrawn and hardened.

When Larry began the pastorate in Arkansas, the church had an attendance of seventy to one hundred people in Sunday worship and had two thousand dollars in the church bank account. Larry was given a weekly salary of $87.50 after taxes. At the point of his resignation in the ninth month of his pastorate, the church had an attendance of 426, with $60,000 in the church bank account. He still had a weekly salary of only $87.50.

The leaders of the church refused to give Larry a raise, having kept him at a poverty-level income for nine months even after Larry shared the way his family was financially humiliated by his lack of income. The leaders further humiliated him by offering him a $300.00 loan in order to have food in the house and some winter clothes for his children. The leaders further stipulated that they would deduct the repayment of the loan from his present salary.

This was a vicious attack on Larry as a man and as a pastor who had worked tirelessly, at times neglecting his own family and personal life. He saw a church showing remarkable growth and evangelistically reaching a town; and yet, he was refused recognition and support from the very people he had served sacrificially. Psychologically Larry was attacked at the most basic level of self-worth and self-concept, as he had to deal with a strong fear of failure.

This was the emotional and psychological context within which Larry Linam lived on that day in 1980, when Alvin King murdered his daughter. The trauma of the Daingerfield murders hit Larry when he was vulnerable and weak form his personal and spiritual career crisis.

Larry developed some very definite coping styles for dealing with the trauma, and also had to live with the maladaptive coping style of other family members, as they too coped with murder. He used denial of the full reality of the murders by obsessing on how to kill King. He was obsessed with getting justice in his own hands. King's suicide froze this obsession into hardness of heart, since it robbed Larry of the opportunity to have justice by his own hands.

Other family members' style of coping was as maladaptive as Larry's One of them denied the full reality by obsessing on pseudo-spiritual forgiveness and ministry to others who had experienced tragedy. Only two weeks after Gina was killed in the Sunday morning worship service, they began a testimony ministry by speaking in Arkansas. They would passionately tell of the horror and declare that they had forgiven Alvin King and received peace and healing. This was an unimaginable source of inner and relational conflict for Larry. Here we have Larry obsessed with finding a way to kill Alvin King by his own hands, sitting in church after church, week after week hearing others proclaim how they had been able to forgive Larry's daughter's murderer.

The early trauma events kept Larry in the midst of the characteristics and behaviors of posttraumatic stress syndrome, as they were reinforced by a series of repetitive traumas.

The trauma took its toll as Larry became divorced several years after Gina's murder. Larry, still carrying the unresolved pain and grief, remarried, and returned to pastoral ministry, only to be traumatized again by having this marriage end in bitter conflict with those who slandered him and attempted to destroy his ministry.

Event after event, situation after situation, all compiled to keep confirming Larry's distorted, pain-produced thinking that somehow had caused his daughter's death by being out of God's will. Each additional traumatizing event seemed to reinforce what the experience with the group therapy counselor in Tyler in 1980 had taught Larry. "No one can help me." Such was the state of mind of the man who sat down with me to tell his story in 1999.

In the days ahead, as our counseling continued, Larry allowed himself to own the full reality of the traumas he had experienced. He confronted his anger at himself and God. He allowed himself to fully grieve and then accept the losses he had experienced in his life. Larry allowed himself to let go of the false guilt he had carried in falsely believing God had allowed Gina's death as a result of his resignation from the church in Lockesburg. A misguided and theologically confused pastor friend had told Larry that the murder of his daughter could be God's judgment on him for rebellion in his ministry. Larry had withdrawn emotionally into nineteen years of self-guilt.

The "stinking thinking" had to be relinquished and the reality of God's comfort in real grieving had to be accepted. Larry Linam has learned to accept the truth of God's Word, which says, "Blessed be the god and Father of our Lord Jesus Christ, the father of mercies and God of all comfort, who comforts us in all our affliction so that we will be able to comfort those who are in any affliction with the comfort with which we ourselves are comforted by God." (2 Corinthians 1: 3-4) This is now one of Larry's life goals, to help comfort you with the comfort he himself has received from the God of all comfort.

PERSONAL TESTIMONY OF
JEFF LINAM

June 22, 1980, was a day that I can only vaguely remember in any great detail. There are a few details I can recall such as Gina lying on the floor and myself tripping over the arm of the old man who was lying to the left of where we were sitting on the back pew, but few other details. This testimony that God has given me is not about recalling those painful memories that occurred on that day but rather one of learning to walk with God and learning to overcome circumstances that life often presents with or without our permission. This testimony is not about defeat but rather one of victory that can only be found in our Savior and Lord Jesus the Christ. The Scripture says it this way in Romans 8:28-29, *"And we know that in all things God works for the good of those who love Him, who have been called according to his purpose. For those God foreknew He also predestined to be conformed to the likeness of His Son...."* These verses sum up what God has done in my life in the years following that day.

In the following years after that day, we moved to Pittsburg, Texas, where I began my schooling. Most of the years in elementary school are pretty much a blur except for the fourth grade. It was then that the nightmares and isolating behavior began. I don't recall many of the things my mom has told me about, such as coming home from school and going to my room and just crying rather than going out to play or watch television. However, I do recall the last nightmare I would have prior to going to a psychiatrist. It was very vivid and lifelike. I clearly recall every detail of that dream. The setting of the dream was in my room in the house we lived in while attending Cross Roads Church in Pittsburg. In my dream, something awakened me from my sleep. I got out of bed and began to walk down the hall of the house that led into the living room. As I entered the living room, I looked on the couch, and there lay my sister Gina. As I looked at her, she got up from the couch, walked over to me and began to hug me. In the dream I knew that she was dead and that this was not possible. I was terrified and crying as she was hugging me. The fear within the dream caused me to awaken from sleeping and I found myself with the same fear from the dream. I was scared and crying as I quickly ran to my parents' room, looking over my left shoulder and thinking, "What if she is really down there?" We then began going to get help from two Christian psychiatrists who could finally diagnose me as being suicidal. I was a kid who had many emotions and did not know how to deal with them.

Being raised in a Christian home with a dad who was a pastor and a mother who was a pastor's wife, I was taught the Bible and all the stories in the Old and New Testaments. I knew who God the Father, God the Son, and God the Holy Spirit were and that they were all powerful, all knowing, and ever present. Taking this knowledge, I can recall sitting in the tub one evening crying and confused, looking for some rationale as to why Gina had to die. I asked my mom a question that I still have no clear answer to that is pleasing to my mind, "Mom, if God is everywhere, all knowing, and all powerful, that means He was there when Gina was shot. He knew it would happen and had the ability to stop it but did not. Why did He choose to let this happen to us?" This question would follow me throughout my life, and God would eventually confront me with this years later.

In 1989, we moved to the small, central west Texas town of Cisco. While in the eighth grade, I participated in athletics because I had a desire to be accepted by the other guys and also because of the influence of a certain coach. As a teacher/coach, I have tried to follow the example that he provided during my years at Cisco ISD. I decided to continue playing football and to participate in track although I continued to be the average person. I was not big, strong, or fast, weighing only 155 pounds and standing 5'10" tall. As a part of the JV squad we would very often run the offense of the opposing team, which meant we got sacrificed to the starting varsity defense. I kept working hard, running track, lifting weights, and learning to overcome obstacles that are common to all student athletes.

Just prior to my junior year I finally began to mature a little bit physically, and all the hard work began to pay off. I made the varsity football team as the starting split end/wide receiver and competed on the varsity track team. The honors and rewards for all the hard work would eventually come my senior year. I made the All-State team as wide receiver in football and was recruited by several colleges before signing with Cisco Junior College. In track, I was the anchor leg for our 1600 meter relay team which made it to the state meet in Austin for the first time in school history (we ran a time of 3:23). My favorite race was the 100 meter dash in which my fastest time was 10:58 seconds. While these accomplishments are worth mentioning, they are a far cry from what I consider to be the best thing to come out of my high school years.

October 15, 1992, I would ask Wendy to be my girlfriend, and she would eventually become my wife. Earlier I made mention of learning to overcome obstacles that would come my way, and one of the biggest obstacles was learning to deal with the divorce of my parents. Instead of turning to God, friends or parents, I turned much of my attention to Wendy. Wendy and I were married on April 2, 1994. Just to clarify, my marriage to Wendy was a wonderful blessing and I am so fortunate to have had that opportunity. I was a senior and she was a sophomore. We now have three wonderful children, Blake (15), Cameron (10), and Allison (5). Looking back on those days I contribute our successful marriage to three main points: 1) keeping Jesus number one in all things, 2) not fighting about money because fighting will not make you any richer, and 3) having a sense of humor and being able to laugh at yourself.

Throughout my life, I had always tried to make sense of why the events of June 22, 1980, took place and tried to do so with a Christian attitude. I had always called myself a follower of Christ Jesus even though many times I did not walk the walk. I had read most of the Bible and had a knowledge of who, what, why, and where's in the Word but often struggled to actually apply much of it, especially if it countered my selfish desires. The events of June 22, 1980, would enter my mind less and less as the years progressed, but when they did, I often had acts of hatred and rage enter my mind and body that would cause me to act out. I would often blame God for what happened and I would make comments like, "I hope the man who did this burns in Hell," and/or, "If he were alive I would choke the very life out of his body and have no remorse whatsoever." That was just how I felt and I certainly had no problem in making that known to anyone who wanted to listen if the subject ever came up. After all, I certainly felt the attitude and comments were well justified. Who would blame me? They would feel the same if the shoe was on the other foot. The reasoning and feelings I had were those of natural humanness and perfectly acceptable to everyone who had a sound mind, or so I thought, believing everyone would agree with me.

You know, one of the lessons I have learned in my life is that when an event occurs like the one in Daingerfield, many times we do not get over it but rather learn to deal with the situation as it is. The hurt does not go away nor does it become less; I just learned to deal with it as the years passed. As I began to read the article clippings and letters concerning the event of June 22, 1980, it was much like ripping open a wound and pouring salt into it. Instantly, the intense hurt, rage, anger, and hatred that had built up over the years came to me flooding my mind, body, emotions, spirit, and every other facet of my being. The memories become vivid which then led to a trail of hot tears. As I had done many times before, I began to curse the man who had killed my sister, hoping he was burning in the hottest parts of hell and getting what he justly deserved. The only regret I had at that point was that I was not the one who would have had the privilege of sending him there. As I continued to read the newspaper clippings, the anger and rage grew, my cries became more passionate, and I am sure my blood pressure was well beyond the normal range. I cried over and over how much I hated this person and then I experienced something that could only cause my anger to become greater than it ever had. In 1Kings 19:11-13 the Bible states, *"The Lord said, Go out and stand on the mountain in the presence of the Lord, for the Lord is about to pass by. Then a great and powerful wind tore the mountains apart and shattered the rocks before the Lord, but the Lord was not in the wind. After the wind there was an earthquake, but the Lord was not in the earthquake. After the earthquake came a fire, but the Lord was not in the fire. And after the fire came a gentle whisper. When Elijah heard it, he pulled his cloak over his face and went out and stood at the mouth of the cave. Then a voice said to him, What are you doing here, Elijah?*

Much like Elijah heard the gentle whisper of God, I too heard a gentle voice that was neither loud nor demanding. The voice I heard was audible although no one else would have heard it had they been there. This voice, I thought, would surely bring comfort during my time of trial and tribulation, but it did not. It only brought a message, one that did not comfort me but rather ticked me off more than I already was. The voice I heard brought the following message,

"Jeff, you need to forgive him."

"What!!!? You cannot be serious. Perhaps you have forgotten what this man did? Forgive him?" This was not the message I was seeking. I wanted everyone to agree with me, to tell me that what I thought was OK and understandable, not to be told that I was not doing what needed to be done. The anger became greater as I began to reason with God on why Al King did not deserve my forgiveness. "Forgive him, there's no way!"

How dare God ask me to do such a thing! "I will not, I cannot forgive him. He does not deserve my forgiveness." There I was on my knees, crying with a hurt I had never experienced. The voice came to me once more, "Jeff, you did not deserve my forgiveness."

"What's that supposed to mean? What do you mean I did not deserve your forgiveness?"

Then it was revealed to me in a very real way. It was my sin that put His Son on the cross that day. All the sins I have ever committed were the reason He died. He died because of me. I had always called Jesus my personal Saviour but had not fully understood that concept until that moment when God had revealed it to me. The realization of this had caused me to be speechless. I did not know how to respond. After a few moments of thinking about what I had heard, I began to pray to the One who had just moments ago directed me to forgive the man who had caused so much hurt. This was my prayer,

"Lord, I have no desire to forgive this man. You know my heart; I hate this person so much. However, I love you and have every desire to please you. If you want me to forgive this person, you will have to do it because I cannot."

I continued to pray this prayer multiple times for seven days. On the following Saturday night as I was taking a bath, I began to cry and said a prayer I will never forget. "Lord, forgive me for my sin of unforgiveness. I now forgive Al King for what he did to my family and if there is any way possible, please do not condemn him to hell for this."

There is no doubt that the Lord did something in my mind and life that only He could do. I learned the difference between hating the sin or act rather than the person who commits it. Just to be clear, I believe that it is appointed to man to die once and then face the judgment. If Al King is in hell, it is because he did not accept Jesus Christ as his Savior; and when he died by his own hands, his fate was sealed at that point. I learned throughout this experience that while Al King was not able to benefit from my forgiveness, I could! I did not realize that the hate, rage, and anger that I had carried for so long were drying up my bones physically, emotionally and spiritually. I released that anger into the hands of a loving God who indeed was long suffering with me during this process.

Proverbs 17:22 says it this way, "*A cheerful heart is good medicine, but a crushed spirit dries up the bones.*"

This is not a story of sadness but of victory in Jesus, of being an overcomer of evil and of learning to lean on God in order to do His will. Many times people know the word of God but have trouble in actually applying it to their lives. We are living in the last days prior to the return of Jesus Christ to get His bride, the true church, and many of these believers have issues of unforgiveness that need to be dealt with. The Word of God is very clear on this issue:

Ephesians 4:23 *"Be kind and compassionate to one another, forgiving each other, just as Christ God forgave you."*

Luke 11:4 – *"Forgive us our sins, for we also forgive **everyone** who sins against us. And lead us not into temptation."*

My challenge for you is to become more like Christ in every aspect of your walk with Him. Does God actually desire for us to forgive those who wrong us? Even those who wish us harm? We must always look to the Word for those answers and it is very clear; yes, we must forgive everyone. I know this is easier said than done, so my request for you is to simply speak your heart to the Father and make your desire known to live a life that is pleasing to Him. Ask Him to take control of the situation and your mind, heart, emotions, and life. He will do a mighty work in you that you would not be able to do yourself. I am not saying that in seven days, as it was in my case for this situation, that you will have reached the state of forgiveness, but when you show a desire to live for God, He will come running with open arms to do a work in your life. My desire is to allow God to use all parts of my life for His glory and to reach and influence as many people as I possibly can before He comes again.

What Satan meant for destruction, Jesus is going to use against him and it is my hope and prayer that I will be a vessel which God will use. God Bless!

Jeff Linam